A SPECIAL PUBLICATION OF THE
ANNALES DU SERVICE DES ANTIQUITÉS DE L'ÉGYPTE

WALL PAINTINGS OF
THE TOMB OF NEFERTARI

WALL PAINTINGS OF
THE TOMB OF NEFERTARI

SCIENTIFIC STUDIES
FOR THEIR CONSERVATION

FIRST PROGRESS REPORT

JULY, 1987

A JOINT PROJECT OF

THE EGYPTIAN ANTIQUITIES ORGANIZATION

AND

THE GETTY CONSERVATION INSTITUTE

COORDINATING EDITOR
Miguel Angel Corzo
The Getty Conservation Institute

EDITORIAL BOARD
Gamal Moukhtar
Former Chairman
The Egyptian Antiquities Organization

SCIENTIFIC BOARD
Saleh Ahmed Saleh
Feisal A. Esmael
Omar El Arini
Kamal Barakat

Photography of site, tomb and murals by Guillermo Aldana for the Getty Conservation Institute. Design by Zempel Group, Inc.

ISBN 0-89236-129-8

Printed in U.S.A.

CONTENTS

PROJECT MEMBERS   6

INTRODUCTION
Ahmed Kadry and Luis Monreal   8

HISTORY
Gaballa Ali Gaballa   10

HISTORY
Mahmoud Maher-Taha   18

ARCHAEOLOGY
Gamal Moukhtar   24

PREVIOUS ENDEAVORS
Ahmed Kadry
Feisal A. Esmael   34

PROJECT BACKGROUND
Miguel Angel Corzo   40

PRELIMINARY RESEARCH RESULTS
Geographic and Geologic Setting
Farouk El-Baz   46
Biological Investigations
Hideo Arai   54
Microflora Investigations
Mokhtar S. Ammar, Kamal Barakat, Essam Hoghanem,
and Asmaa A. El-Deeb   58
Microclimatic Conditions
Feisal A. Esmael   64
Color Measurements
Frank Preusser and Michael Schilling   70
First Report on Analysis of Samples
Frank Preusser   82
Pigments, Plaster and Salt Analyses
Saleh Ahmed Saleh   94
Nondestructive Testing
Modesto Montoto   106
Condition Survey
Paolo Mora, Laura Mora,
Giorgio Capriotti   112

PROJECT MEMBERS

Dr. Ahmed Kadry
Chairman
The Egyptian Antiquities Organization
Cairo, Egypt

Mr. Luis Monreal
Director
The Getty Conservation Institute
Marina del Rey, California, USA

Dr. Gamal Moukhtar
Former Chairman
The Egyptian Antiquities Organization
Cairo, Egypt

Eng. Farrag Abd El Moutaleb
Director of Architectural Affairs
The Egyptian Antiquities Organization
Luxor, Egypt

Eng. Nabil Abd El Samia
Director General of Architectural Affairs
The Egyptian Antiquities Organization
Cairo, Egypt

Mr. Guillermo Aldana
Photographer
Mexico City, Mexico

Prof. Mokhtar S. Ammar
Department of Microbiology
Faculty of Science, Al-Azhar University
Cairo, Egypt

Prof. Hideo Arai
Head, Biology Research Section
Conservation Science Department
Tokyo National Research Institute of
Cultural Property
Tokyo, Japan

Mr. Motawe Balbouch
Director General, Archaeological Sites,
Upper Egypt
The Egyptian Antiquities Organization
Cairo, Egypt

Dr. Kamal Barakat
Director General, Center for Research
and Restoration
The Egyptian Antiquities Organization
Cairo, Egypt

Mr. Giorgio Capriotti
Private Conservator
Rome, Italy

Dr. Miguel Angel Corzo
Director's Office, Project Coordinator
The Getty Conservation Institute
Marina del Rey, California, USA

Ms. Lorenza D'Alessandro
Private Conservator
Rome, Italy

Dr. Omar El Arini
Consultant for Scientific Affairs
National Science Foundation
Cairo, Egypt

Dr. Farouk El Baz
Director, Center for Remote Sensing
Boston University
Boston, Massachusetts, USA

Mrs. Asmaa A. El-Deeb
Researcher,
Center for Research and Restoration
The Egyptian Antiquities Organization
Cairo, Egypt

Dr. Mohamed El Sougayar
Director General of Luxor Antiquities
The Egyptian Antiquities Organization
Luxor, Egypt

Dr. Feisal Abd El Halim Esmael
Scientific Advisor
The Egyptian Antiquities Organization
Cairo, Egypt

Dr. Gaballa Ali Gaballa
Vice Dean, Faculty of Archaeology
Cairo University
Giza, Egypt

Dr. Essam H. Ghanem
Lecturer of Microbiology
Faculty of Science, Al-Azhar University
Giza, Egypt

Dr. Hanl A. Hamroush
Department of Geology
Cairo University
Giza, Egypt

Dr. B. Issawi
Ministry of Petroleum
Cairo, Egypt

Prof. Modesto Montoto
Head, Department of Petrology
University of Oviedo
Oviedo, Spain

Mr. Paolo Mora
Former Chief Conservator
Istituto Centrale di Restauro
Rome, Italy

Mme. Laura Mora
Private Conservator
Rome, Italy

Dr. Shawki Nakhla
Director General of Restoration Section
The Egyptian Antiquities Organization
Cairo, Egypt

Mr. Mohammed Nasr
Chief Inspector
The Egyptian Antiquities Organization
Thebes West
Luxor, Egypt

Dr. Frank Preusser
Director, Scientific Program
The Getty Conservation Institute
Marina del Rey, California, USA

Dr. Saleh Ahmed Saleh
Chairman, Department of Conservation
Faculty of Archaeology, Cairo University
Cairo, Egypt

Mr. Michael Schilling
Assistant Scientist
The Getty Conservation Institute
Marina del Rey, California, USA

Dr. Wafa Seddia
Scientific Director, Pharaonic Sites
The Egyptian Antiquities Organization
Cairo, Egypt

INTRODUCTION

Ahmed Kadry and Luis Monreal

The wall paintings of the tomb of Nefertari have interested scholars, scientists, and the public since their discovery by Ernesto Schiaparelli in 1904 because of their historical importance and exceptional aesthetic value. Their precarious state and the imminent danger of their further decay and eventual ultimate loss have also been the concern of the conservation community.

This publication presents the efforts undertaken since September 1986 to study, research, analyze, and determine a course of action for the emergency consolidation and final conservation treatment of the tomb.

The Egyptian Antiquities Organization and the Getty Conservation Institute, sharing a common concern for the preservation of the cultural heritage, decided to initiate a joint project to find the best possible course of action given the frail state of the wall paintings and urgent need to rescue them from further deterioration. For this purpose a team of Egyptian and foreign specialists from many disciplines was invited by both organizations to participate in this important task. The project began by studying an enhanced digital image taken from a satellite to try to better understand the geology of the Luxor region and specifically that of the Valley of the Queens on the west bank of the Nile. Biological, chemical, physical, and conservation studies were integrated into the total methodology to ensure the success of the work. The papers presented here describe the progress of work undertaken to date.

The Egyptian Antiquities Organization and the Getty Conservation Institute are aware that these are only the first steps and that further, more intensive work is still required. It is our hope that this first progress report will elicit the interest of all involved in the conservation of cultural treasures and of the Nefertari wall paintings in particular.

HISTORY

Nefertari: For Whom the Sun Shines

Gaballa Ali Gaballa

With the advent of the thirteenth century B.C. Egypt began a new phase in her ancient history. Pramesse, chief minister of the state, Deputy of His Majesty in the South and North, and a native of the eastern delta, ascended the throne as pharaoh Rameses I and founded the Nineteenth Dynasty. His brief reign ushered in the Ramesside era, which lasted more than two centuries, c. 1295-1069 B.C. Rameses I's title, *mon-pehty-re* (Enduring is the might of Re) is closely modeled on the title *neb-pehty-re* (Lord of the might of Re), adopted by his distant ancestor Ahmose, champion of the war of liberation and inaugurator of the Eighteenth Dynasty. The new era begun by Rameses was expressed even more explicitly at the coronation of Seti I, his son and successor. Early in his reign Seti took the title *wehem-msut* (Born again), signaling a new beginning. He and his son Rameses II restored to the country its vitality and prestigious position among its neighbors.

During the reign of Seti and the early years of Rameses II's long rule Egypt pursued an offensive policy toward Syria and Palestine

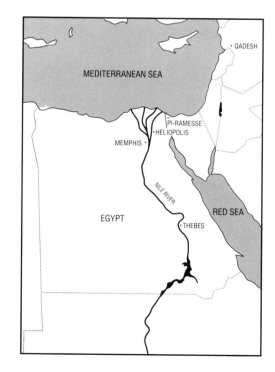

Figure 1. Map of Egypt showing some of the most important sites related to Rameses II and Nefertari.

Figure 3. The Valley of the Queens, on the West bank of the Nile, where the tomb of Queen Nefertari is located.

Figure 2. (opposite) Rameses II embarked on vast building projects and restored to the country its prestigious position.

Figure 4. The most famous and certainly the greatest of Rameses II's temples in Nubia is that of Abu Simbel. The four seated colossi measure about 20 meters in height.

Figure 5. The rock Temple of Hathor was also dedicated to Nefertari, an honor not accorded any other Egyptian queen.

to regain territories lost at the end of the Eighteenth Dynasty. In spite of the strong resistance of their rivals, the Hittites of Anatolia, the Egyptians launched a series of vigorous campaigns, which achieved considerable success. Egypt regained full control of Palestine and dominated vast territories of Syria. In Rameses II's twenty-first regnal year, c. 1259 B.C., a "good treaty of peace and brotherhood" was concluded between Egypt and Hatti. Fourteen years later the peace treaty was sealed, in typical Near Eastern fashion, by Rameses' marriage to a Hittite princess.

At the same time an unprecedented and ambitious program of building, restoring, and renovating was launched. Massive temples and huge monuments were constructed across the entire length and breadth of Egypt and in Nubia and Palestine. In the eastern delta, on the ruins of Avaris, the capital of the Hyksos, sprang Pi-ramesse (Great of Victories), to rival venerable Memphis and glorious Thebes and to become the official royal residence for the Ramesside period. Gold mines were explored, and quarries were opened. In the Theban necropolis new burial grounds were found for the queens and royal children. This area is currently known as the Valley of the Queens, and it is here that the tomb of Nefertari is located.

Although we know much about Rameses II's parents and even grandparents we know very little about Nefertari's parentage. Nowhere in the hundreds of inscriptions related to her is she given any hereditary royal title such as *sat-nesu* (king's daughter) or *senet-nesu* (king's sister), clearly indicating that she was not of royal descent. Her epithet, *merit-mut* (beloved of [the goddess] Mut), may point to a Theban origin for her family. Although of nonroyal blood, her parents (whose names are not known) must have been associated in some way to the court. This connection is proven by Nefertari's elevation to the sublime position of queen and by her title *iret-pat* (hereditary noble[woman]), which was usually borne by women of high society. It was, however, not unprecedented for a king to marry a commoner. Amenophis III married Teye, whose parents were of nonroyal lineage and yet who became one of the most influential queens of the Eighteenth Dynasty.

Scholars believe that Nefertari's marriage to Rameses occurred before he ascended to the throne. In the great Abydos' *Inscription dédicatoire* the king recollects how at his investiture as prince regent his father, Seti I, bestowed on him extensive authority and a

Figure 6. Genealogical relationships of Rameses II and Nefertari.

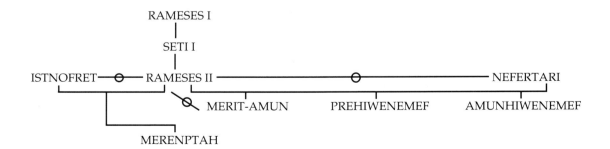

harem. "He [Seti I] furnished me with a household of the royal harem, like the beauties of the palace; he chose for me wives." In his shrine at Gebel el-Silsileh, securely dated to the first year of his reign, are scenes depicting Rameses and Nefertari officiating before many deities. Their eldest son, Amunhiwenemef, is represented several times on the walls of the forecourt of the temple of Beit el-Wali in Nubia, which was erected in the early years of Rameses' reign. These and other indications prove that Nefertari and Rameses were married perhaps six to eight years before his coronation. As the king is thought to have been between twenty and twenty-five years old at his accession and assuming that Nefertari was his age or slightly younger, she must have been only a teenager at her marriage.

From the outset Nefertari enjoyed the signal honor of being the chief queen among Rameses' several wives. As such she bore the official titles *hemet-nesu-weret* (great royal wife), *nebet-tui* (lady of the Two Lands [Egypt]), and *henet-tui* (mistress of the Two Lands). Being the chief consort of the divine king she was also given religious titles such as *hemet-neter* (god's wife), *mut-neter* (god's mother), and *weret-heneru* (chief of the harem [of Amun]). In addition endearing epithets expressing the king's affection were also accorded her: *weret-hesut* (rich of praise), *nebet-iamt* (lady of charm), *beneret-mrut* (sweet of love), *nefert-her* (beautiful of face).

Nefertari was the mother of six or seven sons and daughters, among them Rameses' first born, Prince Amunhiwenemef, who was designated as heir apparent to the throne but died young. She also bore Prince Prehiwenemef who accompanied his father in the notorious battle of Qadesh. He and Prince Meryatum (Rameses' sixteenth son and High Priest of Re in Heliopolis) died during their father's life. Of her daughters Merit-Amun became the king's chief consort during the middle years of his reign. She also died before her father and was buried in tomb 68 in the Valley of the Queens, next to that of her mother. As none of Nefertari's children seems to have outlived their father, it was a son of her rival, Queen Istnofret, namely Merenptah, who succeeded Rameses to the throne.

Pictorial and textual evidence shows that of all Rameses' wives, Nefertari played the most prominent role in the realm. She always appeared with the king in public, on state occasions, and in religious ceremonies. She was with him when, in his first year, he sailed upstream from Pi-ramesse to Thebes, passing through Heliopolis and Memphis where he was acclaimed as sole monarch. While in Thebes she joined him in the celebrations of the Festival of Opet and witnessed the investiture of Nebwenenef as high priest of Amun. Her images are always shown next to those of her husband's in the temples of Luxor, Karnak, and Abu Simbel. The little rock temple of Hathor at Abu Simbel was dedicated to her, an honor not accorded to any other Egyptian queen, perhaps with the exception of Teye.

Nefertari's public role was not only limited to domestic matters but extended to embrace the international scene. After the conclusion of the peace treaty between Rameses and the Hittites, Nefertari sent a letter of greeting to Pudukhepa, the Hittite queen. It reads:

> Thus says Naptera [Nefertari], the great queen of Egypt: "To Pudukhepa, the great queen of Hatti, my sister, speak thus: 'With me your sister, all goes well; with my country all goes well. With you, my sister, may all go well; with your country may all go well. Behold now, I have noted that you, my sister, have written to me, to enquire after my well being. And that you have written to me about the relationship

of good peace and brotherhood in which the great king, the king of Egypt [now stands] with his brother, the great king, the king of Hatti.

" 'May the sun god [of Egypt] and storm god [of Hatti] bring you joy; and may the sun god cause the peace to be good and give good brotherhood to the great king, the king of Egypt, with his brother the great king, the king of Hatti, forever. And [now] I am in friendship and sisterly relations with my sister, the great queen [of Hatti], now and forever.' "

In the year 24, c. 1255 B.C., Nefertari accompanied Rameses on his journey to Nubia to participate in the dedication of her small temple at Abu Simbel. This act seems to have been the queen's last major public performance. She was now in her midforties, and she gracefully faded from the scene. As her mummy was never recovered, the cause and manner of her death are not known; yet after thirty-three centuries Nefertari's memory lives on, her gracious countenance radiating from the scenes depicted on temple walls and in her tomb. Her slim shapely figure, beautiful profile with its delicate features, the elegance of her dress and posture, will always be the envy of many a woman.

References

Desroches-Noblecourt, C., and C. Kuentz.1968. *Le petit temple d'Abou-Simbel.* Vols. I, II. Le Caire.

Faulkner, R.O. "Egypt: from the Inception of the Nineteenth Dynasty to the Death of Rameses III." In I.E.S. Edwards et al., *The Cambridge Ancient History*, 3: 217-51.

Goedicke, H. and G. Thausing. 1971. *Nefertari: Documentation of the Tomb and Its Decoration.* Graz.

Helck, W. 1982. "Nofretere." In *Lexikon der Ägyptologie,* 4: 518-19. Wiesbaden.

Kitchen, K. A. 1982. *Pharaoh triumphant: The life and times of Ramesses II.* Warminster.

Langdon, S. and A. H. Gardiner. 1920. "The Treaty of Alliance between Hattusili, king of the Hittites and the Pharaoh Ramesses II of Egypt." *Journal of the Egyptian Antiquities Organization:* 179-205.

Marwan, N. Z. 1982. "Queen Nefertari: Wife of Ramesses and her monuments." M.A. dissertation, Cairo University. In Arabic.

Schmidt, J. D. 1970. *Ramesses: A chronological structure of his reign.* Baltimore and London.

HISTORY

The Considerable and Unique Position of Nefertari

Mahmoud Maher-Taha

Although much has been said and written about Queen Nefertari, her role in the events of her reign remains rather obscure. The inscriptional material from her reign reveals some clues regarding her important position. Her political role is reflected by the epithets: *hnwt-smꜥ–Mhw* (mistress of the south and the north) and *nbt-t3wy* (lady of the Two Lands). Both are parallel to common royal epithets (king of upper and lower Egypt) and (lord of Two Lands) that are legal expressions of the king's power to rule Egypt. Nefertari is also the only Egyptian queen to have the royal epithet *nbt-t3w-nbw* (mistress of all lands). Another epithet, however, describes her as "appeasing the gods." This expression refers to kings and states their adherence to and support of the ritual requirements of cults.

Figure 1. This relief shows the only instance in which a queen is represented in a military scene.

In addition to her epithets, there are a considerable number of indications suggesting that Nefertari was not just an ordinary queen but rather an important queen during a significant period. These indications are traced through the following archaeological facts:

1. Nefertari's first appearance is on the stela at Gebel Silsileh, in the royal shrine of Rameses II. The depiction of the shrine shows Rameses II and Nefertari performing religious activities before a number of deities. This stela was inscribed in the first regnal year and indicates that Nefertari was already married to Rameses II before his accession ca. 1290 B.C.

    It is known that King Rameses II began his reign as coregnant with his father Seti I; this period lasted about seven years. Because the Ramessides home was in the north, Rameses II and Seti I made strenuous attempts to improve their situation in the south. They did so through the marriage of Rameses II to Nefertari; for this

Figure 2. Six standing colossi face the Temple of Nefertari at Abu Simbel. No other wife of Rameses is ever represented in the same size as the king.

reason Rameses II was keen on appearing with her in public. Another explanation suggests that she influenced his position.

2. Another inscription from the first year of Rameses II's reign, registered in his tomb, pertains to the appointment of Nebwenemef II as a high priest of Amun. The awarding of this high rank took place in the presence of Rameses II and Nefertari. It is the first time that we see the participation of a queen in state affairs, except for Nefertiti.

3. The first half of Rameses II's reign is filled with military activities, primarily in Asia. In the regnal year 21 (ca. 1270 B.C.) after the Battle of Qadesh, Rameses II and Hattusilis III signed a treaty and formed an alliance, thus providing us with a specific date for a comparative chronology. Fragments of a letter from the archive of Boghazkoy include congratulations on the peace treaty addressed to the Queen of Khatti by Queen Nefertari. Therefore the participation of Nefertari in foreign politics is unparalleled by any other queen.

Figure 3. Rameses II faces the sacred bark of Amun-Re; Nefertari is behind him.

4. As far as we know, none of the Egyptian queens had a temple dedicated to her jointly with a goddess, as is the case with Nefertari at Abu Simbel. Six standing colossi face this temple. The colossi are the same size; four represent the king and two represent the queen. There are three on each side of the central doorway (figure 2). No other wife of Rameses II is ever represented in the same size as the king.

5. In the hypostyle hall of the small temple of Abu Simbel, the reliefs on the walls on either side of the entrance have a representation of Rameses II, accompanied by Nefertari, standing behind him, smiting a Lybian in the presence of Re-Harakhty on the north side, and a Nubian in the presence of Amun-Re on the south side (figure 1). It is the only instance in which a queen is represented in a military scene, behind the king.

6. In the hypostyle hall of the great temple of Abu Simbel, a scene depicts the sacred bark of Amun-Re carried by priests. Rameses II faces the bark and Nefertari is behind him (figure 3).

7. On the second pylon of the Ramesseum, the mortuary temple of Rameses II at Luxor-West, the feasts of Min are depicted. In the fourth episode of these feasts, Nefertari participates in a ceremonial dance taking the role of *sm3ᶜjt* beside the white bull, *K3-hd*, that represents the god Min. Nefertari is the only queen in the history of Egypt

who figures in a case such as this. During Rameses III's reign, artists copied the same scenes in the temple of Medinet Habu (also at Luxor-West), leaving the cartouche of Rameses III's favorite queen empty. This probably means that there was no other queen who was worthy of taking a similar role.

It is believed that Nefertari died in about the 24th year of Rameses II's reign, before the First Jubilee in the year 30. A number of stelae that record the jubilees of the regnal years 30, 37 and 40 are among the inscriptions of Rameses II at Gebel Silsileh. In the upper part of each stela, Rameses II, followed by his son *Hᶜ-m-w3-st*, is offering the image of *Maᶜ-at* to Ptah, Amun-Re, and Sobek. The fact that none of Rameses II's other known queens is represented in these stelae demonstrates the unique position of Nefertari among Egyptian queens.

References

CEDEA Archives (Search Salle -H).

Desroches-Noblecourt C. and C. Kuentz. 1968. *Le petit temple D'Abou-Simbel.* Vols. I, II. Le Caire.

Goedicke, H. and G. Thausing. 1971. *Nefertari: Documentation of the Tomb and Its Decoration.* Graz.

Kitchen, K.A. 1982. *Ramsès II, le pharaon triomphant.* Paris.

Lalouette. 1981. *L'empire des Ramsès.* Paris.

Loyrette and Maher-Taha. 1979. *Les fêtes du Dieu Min.* CS No. 36, CEDEA. Le Caire.

Sethe. 1907. *Die Berufung eines Hohen priesters des Amon unter Ramesses II.* ZÄS 44.

Valbelle. 1985. *Les ouvriers de la tombe.* Bd'E 96. Le Caire.

ARCHAEOLOGY

Gamal Moukhtar

In the far southwest of the Theban necropolis lies the Valley of the Queens, which the ancient Egyptians called "the place of beauty." In this small valley were buried the wives and children of the royal family during the Nineteenth and Twentieth dynasties (the Ramesside period). Most of the tombs are unfinished or not inscribed or decorated. The joint expedition of the Egyptian Center of Documentation and the French National Center of Scientific Research are presently excavating and attempting to identify them.

The earliest tomb from the Nineteenth Dynasty in this valley is that of Queen Set Re, wife of Rameses I, but the most impressive tomb is that belonging to Queen Nefertari, favorite wife of Rameses II. Unfortunately because of salt damage and considerable paint loss this tomb has been closed to the general public since its discovery in 1904 by Ernesto Schiaparelli, head of the Italian Archaeological Expedition to the Valley of the Queens. This tomb was—as nearly all the tombs of this valley—entirely plundered during ancient times.

The representations of Queen Nefertari in her tomb introduce her to us as a pretty woman of charm and grace. She possesses a beautiful face and slim-waisted figure. Her profile is elaborated, her hand gestures delicate, and her posture majestic. She is depicted entering the afterworld as a lovely wife and splendid queen.

The tomb of Queen Nefertari is, as are other tombs in the Valley of the Queens, relatively small, compared with tombs in the Valley of the Nobles. No tomb in western Thebes or in the whole of Egypt, however, is comparable to it in its artistic superiority and fascination.

The tomb was hewn at a depth reaching about 12 m in poor quality limestone rock. Ancient artists were obliged to cover the wall surfaces with layers of plaster, which they skillfully carved and painted in low relief. Paintings also cover the ceiling of the tomb, which represents a deep blue sky with yellow stars. The wall paintings include religious and funeral scenes, magical formulas, and chapters from the Book of the Dead.

In spite of the considerable destruction and loss, the tomb is full of rich and brilliant colors with exceptionally vivid physical depictions and diverse hieroglyphics. New artistic techniques were used in the modeling of figures by shading with pigment and in arrangement of compositions. The splendid paintings of this tomb reflect the genius and skill of the artists and draftsmen working during the Ramesside artistic renaissance.

The rock salt that has crystallized behind the plaster layer and pushed it outward is responsible for the damage and losses sustained by the tomb, especially in the burial chamber. The tomb has suffered notably since its clearing eighty-three years ago. The Egyptian Center of Documentation, aware of the danger, began in 1965 the complete scientific documentation of the tomb, which included photographic, architectural, line drafting, archaeological, and epigraphic registration.

Although several attempts were conducted and serious studies and experiments were carried out aimed at treating the damage, stopping the deterioration of the paintings, and preserving the whole tomb, none proved successful and no project was approved or accepted. Nevertheless, the tomb of Nefertari, in spite of the damage, is still pleasant to the eye and inspires admiration.

Figure 1. Plan and cross-section of Nefertari's tomb.

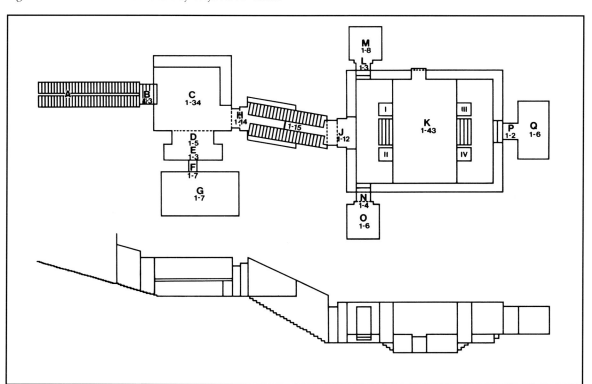

Figure 2. Queen Nefertari, favorite wife of Rameses II, is represented with delicate hand gestures and majestic posture.

Figure 3. The tomb contains an entry passage and several architectural units gathered in two complexes linked by a descending passageway.

Figure 4. The doorways are decorated and inscribed with the name and titles of Nefertari and with representations of deities.

Figure 5. The cobras are a continuing decoration motif in the tomb.

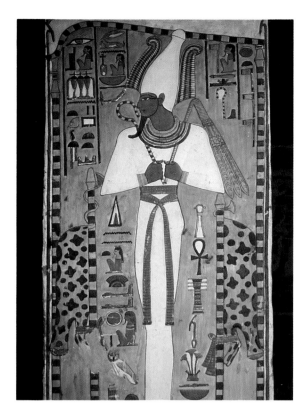

Figure 6. In the rebirth of Osiris, the people saw their own triumph over death.

Figure 7. Anubis, god of embalming, is a guardian of the tomb and of the necropolis.

Figure 8. Horus, son of Isis, was the hawk-headed royal god of Egypt and is seen here with Nefertari.

30

Figure 9. Scene representing the seven sacred cows and a bull with the four steering oars of the sky.

Figure 10. The walls of the burial chamber are mostly decorated with scenes of the Book of the Gates and the Book of the Dead.

Figure 11. Scene depicting Nefertari in the shape of a mummy.

The tomb is formed on an axial plan (see figure 1.) and contains an entry passage and seven architectural units, which vary in size, depth, function, and scope. They are gathered in two complexes linked by a descending corridor. The outer complex is composed of an outside room (antechamber), a recess with a short passage connecting the outside and inside rooms. The inner complex, which is at a lower level, includes a burial chamber (sarcophagus room) connected with two flanking side rooms, and a small inner room.

The entrance is a short descending ramp, about 4.5 m long, with a staircase leading to the actual tomb, through which the dead queen would be transferred to eternal life. The jambs and doorways are decorated and inscribed with the name and titles of Nefertari and with representations of deities, now defaced. The soffit and lintel are decorated with a scene of the setting sun and a frieze of cobras and feathers, which continues inside the tomb.

Although the outside room is considered one of the two main rooms of the tomb, it is notably small and nearly square in shape (5.30 x 5.20 m). It functions as a path to transfer the dead queen toward the monarchy of Osiris, the first stage of the queen's journey to the afterworld. On its walls are scenes representing the queen adoring Osiris, Horus, Anubis, Isis, Maat, and other gods and goddesses and illustrations and inscriptions related to the seventeenth chapter of the Book of the Dead. The entrance to the tomb is through the southern wall of this room, while the corridor leading to the burial chamber is located through its northern wall. A rock-cut bench, with niches below it, projects from the western and northern walls.

A passage in the eastern wall of the outside chamber leads to a recess separating the first room from a side room, oriented toward the east. The walls of the recess, its passage, and the inside room contain scenes depicting Nefertari worshiping or being conducted to the afterworld by various deities. The most interesting scene in the inside room represents the seven sacred cows and the bull with the four steering oars of the sky, symbolizing the world power. Passages from the 94th and 148th chapters of the Book of the Dead are inscribed on the walls.

The corridor, or funerary path, which is about 7m long leads from a staircase to the inner complex. The paintings on both sides of the corridor present Nefertari adoring various gods and goddesses, as well as wild demons and guardian-deities who protect her name. Most inscriptions are related to chapter 151 of the Book of the Dead. The doorway jambs of the burial chamber are inscribed with the name and titles of Nefertari, while the soffit is decorated with a winged Maat. This corridor leads to that part of the tomb where the funeral ceremony was terminated and in which occurred the final transition to the burial chamber.

The burial chamber is a relatively large rectangular room (10.40 x 8.50 m) with four square pillars supporting the ceiling. Two side rooms and a small inner room are accessible from it. The entry walls to the burial chamber are adorned by four goddesses, while the walls are mostly decorated with scenes from the Book of the Gates and the Book of the Dead. The queen is represented passing through nine gates from the domain of Osiris, which are guarded by dreadful demons. On the northern wall of the chamber she is shown before Osiris, Hathor, and Anubis. The four pillars form a kind of shrine to contain her sarcophagus, now lost. The pillars are decorated with the Djed pillar and various deities.

The two side rooms flanking the burial chamber on the west and east are poorly preserved. An interesting scene on the eastern wall of the western side room shows Nefertari in the shape of a mummy. The function of the small inner room and two side rooms is not yet known because of their great obliteration.

It is hoped that through the collaboration of the Egyptian Antiquities Organization and the Getty Conservation Institute the tomb will be saved and visitors from all over the world will be given the opportunity to visit it and admire its artistry, harmony, and elegance.

References

Conservator's Information Center. 1973. *The Tomb of Queen Nefertari.* Warsaw.

Desroches-Noblecourt, C. 1976. *Ramses Le Grand: Catalogue de l'Exposition.* Paris.

Desroches-Noblecourt, C. and C. Kuentz. 1968. *Le petit temple D'Abou- Simbel. Vols. I, II.* Le Caire.

Geodicke, H. and G. Thausing. 1971. *Nefertari: Documentation of the Tomb and Its Decoration.* Graz.

Porter, B. and R. Moss. 1934. *Topographical Bibliography of Ancient Egyptian Hieroglyphic Texts. V Upper Egypt, Sites.* Oxford.

Schiaparelli, E. 1903-20. *Relazione sui Lavori della Missione Archeologica Italiana in Egitto. Vol. 1, Esplorazione della "Valle delle Regine" nella Necropoli di Tebe.*

Smith, W. S. 1958. *The Art and Architecture of Ancient Egypt.* Harmondsworth.

PREVIOUS ENDEAVORS

Ahmed Kadry and Feisal A. Esmael

During the past year the Egyptian Antiquities Organization and the Getty Conservation Institute have collaborated closely in an effort to explore ways of treating the wall paintings in the tomb of Nefertari.

Since its discovery the tomb has been the subject of great interest and grave concern regarding its state of conservation. Because of its rarity and exceptional importance it was extremely difficult to evaluate the countless rescue plans suggested in the past. It is hoped that in the current project the tomb will reach its well-deserved and safest haven. This optimism is justified by the amassed wealth of ideas from many qualified and able sources and by the latest advances in preventive care and conservation measures and materials.

The tomb's problems were initially viewed with the conviction that in restoration lie all desired answers. This perception had persisted and dominated throughout a period of more than forty years. From 1934 to 1977 many restoration experiments were performed with varying degrees of scope, effect, and success. As the need for systematic scientific investigations became apparent, many committees and study groups were formed to assess the tomb's state and to arrive at scientific answers to its core and peripheral problems. Since an awareness of past plans and endeavors was imperative in devising our present work plan and conducting our current operations in the tomb, a review of those endeavors constitutes the main body of this basically introductory and general report.

The tomb has been the subject of a great number of scientifically motivated surveys and exploratory missions, most of which have produced only general memoranda. In this report, only adequately documented and complete treatment surveys will be presented. Appearing in chronological order, these include the following:

1. The United Nations Educational, Scientific, and Cultural Organization (UNESCO) Report, May 1970: "United Arab Republic conservation problems," issued in Paris,

serial number 1914/BMS.RD/CLT.

2. The International Centre for the Study of the Preservation and the Restoration of Cultural Property Report, June 1978: "ICCROM Mission to the Tomb of Queen Nefertari," issued in Rome and marked GT/EA.

3. The Cairo University Report (CUR), July 1980: "Nefertari's Tomb: Signs and agents of damage and methods of their treatment," issued in Cairo, in Arabic.

4. The Canadian Reports, May 1981: "Tomb of Nefertari and its conservation problems," issued in Toronto, Ontario; 1982: "Chemistry and physics in the tomb of Nefertari," *Journal of the Society for the Study of Egyptian Antiquities* 12, no. 1: 9-11; June 1982: "The internal climate of Nefertari," issued in Toronto, Ontario.

5. The Italian Report, June 1983: A text on the survey of the tomb carried out in January 1983 and issued in Aramengo.

The limited scope and general nature of this report require that we focus our discussion on the salient features of the principal investigations.

The UNESCO Report. Presented in two parts as the outcome of a 1970 UNESCO mission to Egypt, this report deals with museums and sites, with special emphasis on the tombs of Bani Hassan and Nefertari. Members of the mission were H. J. Plenderleith, P. Mora, G. Torraca, and G. de Guichen. One of the most far reaching claims of the mission with respect to the tomb of Nefertari was the assertion that "almost no change is detectable. Even in places where the plaster is dangerously detached from the rock wall, no important losses could be found on comparing the original with the pictures taken in 1904." Such a claim was repeated in successive investigations; with present facilities, in particular those of image processing and enhancement, this claim can be quantitatively examined.

The report further states that the tomb of Nefertari was previously visited by two UNESCO missions in 1958 and 1969 and maintains that deterioration in the tomb can be attributed to rain, soluble salts, and dehydration of plaster. The mission's approach to treatment begins by defining the aim of restoration as "mainly to improve adhesion of plaster to the walls, and re-inforce its cohesion strength." For the latter, use of selected fixatives was suggested.

Details of two detachment and repositioning experiments carried out by Egyptian Antiquities Organization personnel in 1958 and 1967 were given. In both, treatment began by consolidating the painted surface, and the manner in which this step was executed may account for the darkening of the treated fragments and should be avoided in current attempts.

The ICCROM Report.   The text presented by Giorgio Torraca was the outcome of ICCROM's 1978 mission in Egypt and deals with deterioration process, conservation and stabilization, work program, and cost estimation.

Deterioration of the tomb of Nefertari was attributed to the slow evaporation of salt-laden water, with subsequent growth of salt crystals and progressive dehydration of the gypsum-based plaster; occasional flooding of the tomb; and rapid, but intermittent growth of salt crystals, during which the gypsum-based mortar is assumed to undergo dehydration during the long dry periods.

Regarding conservation and stabilization the report states that "any attempt to control the growth of salt crystals through total removal of the paintings and creation of an isolation cavity might result in irreparable damage to the paintings and the site as a whole."

Two campaigns of forty to forty-five days each were suggested by the report for the proposed work program of preliminary studies and conservation treatment. Finally the cost of the execution of the program was estimated in 1978 at a total of about U.S. $440,000.

The Cairo University Report (CUR). Prepared by Saleh Ahmed Saleh of Cairo University, the report is an extensive study and may be considered the major local contribution to collective treatment of the tomb of Nefertari.

Of the factors accelerating the tomb's deterioration, CUR principally considers salt-laden rain water, frequent landslides, the microclimate of the tomb, and the poor quality of the limestone forming the mother rock. Following detailed restoration proposals, CUR suggests post-treatment measures involving architectural interventions such as the creation of external slight slopes, sealing the body of the tomb, fitting a double-door airtight entrance to serve as a buffer corridor, and installing protective railings.

The Canadian Reports. The Canadian team undertaking investigations inside the tomb of Nefertari from 1977 to 1981 was composed of T. C. Billard, George Burns, and K. M. Wilson-Yang, members of the archaeometric group of the Department of Chemistry at Toronto University.

The team established three work objectives: (1) to "examine the state of deterioration of the tomb in order to deduce the nature of the most urgent problems and the steps needed for their circumvention," (2) to "perform preliminary photogrammetric experiments to develop a technique suitable for the assessment of the state and rate of deterioration of the Tomb," (3) to "collect small samples for microscopic study of its chemistry for the development of its conservation."

The actual output, however, was confined to microclimatic monitoring. The team arrived at three principal conclusions: (1) "It was discovered that merely entering the Tomb changes the climate noticeably;" (2) "The entry of a person may not only be dangerous to the safety of the Tomb, it will also distort the measurements being made;" (3) "Recent changes of climate in Luxor are causes of concern to us. Specifically since the Aswan Dam construction, precipitation in Luxor area has increased."

Elsewhere in this publication results of the latest microclimatic survey of the tomb are presented and the above claims duly examined (see "Microclimatic Conditions" by Feisal A. Esmael).

The Italian Report. This report presents the outcome of investigations carried out over the period 12-17 January 1983 inside the tomb by two members of the Aramengo Restoration Laboratory, Gian Luigi Nicola and Roberto Arosio, with the supervision and participation of the Egyptian Antiquities Organization. The exploratory campaign principally involved microclimatic measurements and assessment, a general inspection survey of the tomb, and ultraviolet monitoring and examination of wall paintings. Several samples were also taken for analysis, and in situ tests of candidate fixatives were performed.

The Aramengo investigators presented a methodology based on the following premises:

1. Removal of existing salt is not envisaged, which may be exploited as a hard backing, provided that complete outside sealing is secured and crystal growth is halted.

2. No single approach can be safely applied to all areas. Treatment will vary; and in some areas superficial consolidation will be sufficient, in others anchorage of the paint to the underlying wall will be necessary, or third-class stucco techniques may be applied.

This brief review of past rescue endeavors is intended to help future workers avoid evident pitfalls and establish a firmer foundation for current and planned efforts.

PROJECT BACKGROUND

Miguel Angel Corzo

In September 1985 the Egyptian Antiquities Organization and the Getty Conservation Institute began consultations on a program of cooperation that would underline their interest in and dedication to the conservation of the cultural heritage. The two organizations agreed that a joint conservation program, encompassing scientific research and advanced training, would be established. That program would address the conservation of the wall paintings of the Pharaonic period focusing on the tomb of Nefertari.

Under the authority of the Egyptian Antiquities Organization and with the support of the Getty Conservation Institute, a multidisciplinary team of Egyptian and foreign specialists was invited to study, propose, and carry out a conservation treatment of the wall paintings in the tomb. The interdisciplinary approach envisaged will contribute to the field and provide appropriate training for selected Egyptian conservators.

Directed by the Egyptian Antiquities Organization, the program will consist of six basic steps: (1) review of existing documentation, (2) research and analysis, (3) emergency consolidation to secure the wall paintings in the tomb, (4) planning of the final treatment, (5) test of the final treatment, (6) treatment of the wall paintings.

The first four steps, phase one of the program, will have a duration of twelve months. The time span of the last two steps will be determined after the completion of the first phase.

As part of the joint program the Getty Conservation Institute established fellowships to receive Egyptian specialists at the Institute's laboratories to deal with those scientific aspects requiring further training and research. The program also necessitated the establishment of a field laboratory near the tomb. This facility will be provided by the Egyptian Antiquities Organization for the duration of the agreement. The Getty Conservation Institute will furnish and install the laboratory with the necessary scientific equipment as well as supply the scientific field equipment and materials needed for implementing steps 1 through 4 of the work plan.

The program will be developed according to a predetermined schedule and will be extensively documented for future training purposes by both institutions. The program's progress will be evaluated on a regular basis by the Egyptian Antiquities Organization and the Getty Conservation Institute. Visiting consultants, chosen by the Egyptian Antiquities Organization and the Getty Conservation Institute, will be invited on an ad hoc basis to serve as advisors. The Egyptian Antiquities Organization will assign the necessary staff to provide support to the program. A field project coordinator will be jointly appointed by the Egyptian Antiquities Organization and the Getty Conservation Institute. The Egyptian Antiquities Organization will ensure the implementation of all operations, including the availability of documentation as required by the program, access to the site, and assignment to the project of technical personnel chosen with the aim of providing them with advanced training opportunities.

Figure 1. Efficient management systems are also being applied in the development of this project. CPM/PERT diagram is used to determine the progress of the project.

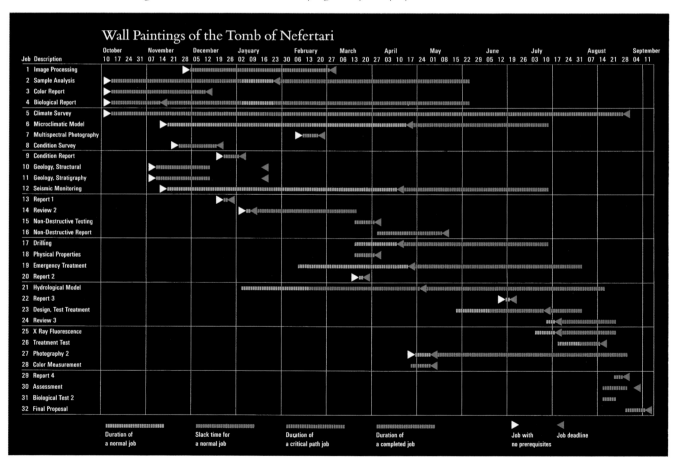

In September 1986 a meeting was held in Cairo to discuss the details of the program. Egyptian and foreign scientists and specialists agreed on the various activities—their scope and sequence—required to study the conservation problems of the wall paintings in the tomb. Areas requiring study were identified and include: the geological setting of the tomb, analysis of salt and plaster samples from the wall paintings, possible biological activity within the tomb, microclimatic monitoring within the tomb, potential uses of non-destructive techniques to detect voids between the plaster and rock, and condition surveys of the wall paintings.

Egyptian and foreign scientists and specialists visited the tomb during the month and began work on these activities. In January 1987 the teams met again in Luxor to discuss their progress and to agree on an emergency consolidation of the wall paintings, which began in April 1987.

Because of the precarious state of the wall paintings of the tomb of Nefertari both institutions intend to proceed promptly and continue with this joint effort for the permanent conservation treatment of the tomb.

These papers present the results of research undertaken to date and are intended as a progress report. Future publications will describe in detail the activities related to the conservation of one of the world's most important cultural treasures.

PRELIMINARY RESEARCH REPORTS

Geographic and Geologic Setting

Farouk El-Baz

This paper is one result of a preliminary survey of the tomb of Queen Nefertari. The survey is part of a study jointly undertaken by the Egyptian Antiquities Organization and the Getty Conservation Institute. Prior to the field survey, conducted on 8-13 September 1986, a Thematic Mapper image of the site and its environs was computer enhanced and photologically analyzed. This resulted in establishing patterns of structure and drainage, which follow three major trends: NE-SW, NW-SE, and E-W. Local topography, however, controls the microdrainage patterns of surface water from occasional rainfall.

Observation within the tomb and two other shallow tombs on either side indicate that the limestone rock is highly jointed. The resulting spaces are filled with fibrous crystals of gypsum at right angles to the joint planes. The content of rock salt in these joints appears to increase with depth. This suggests the possible leaching of rock salt from higher horizons to lower ones, where it recrystallizes behind the plaster layer of the wall paintings. The salt crystals appear to force the plaster layer outward, resulting in severe damage.

The tomb of Nefertari is number 66 in the Valley of the Queens, a small wadi bounded by a high escarpment at the edge of the hills in western Thebes, the ancient name of Luxor. To fully understand the setting of the Valley of the Queens, one is advised to review photographs and images obtained from spacecraft as a prelude to the examination of the larger-in-scale aerial photographs. The best space photographs of the region are those obtained by Gemini XII in 1966, by Landsat satellites starting in 1972, and by the Space Shuttle Large Format Camera (LFC) in 1984.

The hills that surround the Valley of the Queens are part of an extensive plateau that forms the eastern boundary of the Western Desert of Egypt. This boundary also represents the edge of the Nile Valley, which encloses the agricultural strip along the banks of the Nile River.

A study of Gemini XII photographs (Yehia, 1973), established that the region is characterized by dendritic and subdendritic to subtrellis drainage. It also recognized that drainage lineations are controlled by gravity, structure, and/or lithology.

Images obtained by Landsat were used to delineate geographic features of the

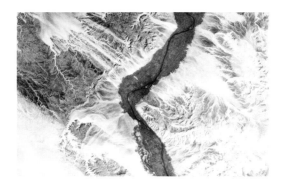

Figure 1. Thematic Mapper image of the Luxor region showing the Thebes Plateau west of the Nile Valley. Major fracture systems and drainage lines are clearly delineated. Bright areas, particularly in the lower left corner, are deposits of sand carried by the wind from farther west.

Figure 2. Enlargement of part of the Thematic Mapper image of the Luxor region showing the scalloped nature of the scarp that forms the western border of the Nile Valley. Most of the drainage lines in the Thebes Plateau trend in a northwesterly direction.

Figure 3. Enlargement of part of the Thematic Mapper image of the Luxor area showing the airport in the lower right corner and road that leads to the tomb of Nefertari on the west side of the Nile (arrow). The escarpment closest to the western bank of the Nile separates the area of the Valley of the Queens from the regional drainage system to the north and west.

Figure 4. Photograph of the southwest edge of the escarpment that bounds the Valley of the Queens, showing part of the highly fractured limestone rock of the Nile Valley fault zone.

region (El-Baz, 1979). Earlier Landsat images were characterized by relatively low ground resolution, about 80 m. Later images obtained by the Thematic Mapper have 30 m resolution. An image of the study area was requested from the Earth Observation Satellite Company. The image, obtained on 22 January 1986 (50069-20746-TMWNO; N26-00 E32-21; path 175, row 42), was specially computer enhanced by the Earth Satellite Corporation of Chevy Chase, Maryland; details from this image are discussed here. The higher-resolution photographs (about 20 m) by the LFC are yet to be studied.

Study of the Thematic Mapper images of the Luxor area (figure 1) indicates that the Thebes Plateau on the west bank of the Nile is characterized by three major fracture systems: (1) the E-W fault system which appears to be the oldest because it is truncated in several places by the two other systems; (2) the NW-SE fault system, emphasized by numerous primary drainage lines and wide valleys; (3) the NE-SW fault system, mainly followed by major escarpments, but also parallel to secondary drainage lines.

These trends reflect the major fracture pattern of the Western Desert of Egypt as previously deduced from studies of space photographs, particularly from the Apollo-Soyuz mission (El-Etr, Moustafar, and El-Baz, 1979).

The Nile Valley in this region follows the NE-SW direction (figure 2). It is clearly evident that the Nile itself occupies a course in the lowest part of the fertile valley; it is unlikely that its water has much to do with the moisture in the Theban hills at higher altitudes.

Closer examination of the environment of the Valley of the Queens shows that the region is controlled by one major fracture parallel to the Nile Valley fault zone. The fracture also shows the distinctive scalloped appearance of other parts of the fault zone as it truncates a protrusion of rock that extends into the Nile Valley (figure 3). This particular setting has resulted in the separation of the region of the Valley of the Queens (along with the area of the temple of Hatshepsut) from the regional drainage pattern to the north and west.

This setting is particularly lucky because it will simplify the establishment of a hydrological model for the region. It may also simplify the potential damming of wadis to minimize the amount of water that reaches the vicinity of the tomb of Nefertari from future occasional rainfall. This would have been much more difficult if the area were fed by the regional drainage pattern.

The rock in which the tomb of Nefertari is located is a clayey limestone, with concoidal fracture. It is very fine grained and highly fractured by several joint systems. The extensive fracturing and jointing appears to be due mainly to the fact that the region is part of the Nile Valley fault zone. Most fractures developed at the time of the Nile Valley formation; more recent fractures and joints, however, are present.

The most pronounced joint system is that which parallels the main escarpment of the Nile Valley. The distances between joints are at times only a few centimeters. All the resulting spaces appear to be filled mainly with gypsum, the crystal growths of which are normal to the joint planes. In most cases the joints themselves are a few millimeters wide, but a few can be measured in centimeters.

The second most pronounced set of joints cuts across the latter joint system, forming a rhomboidal, "baklavalike" pattern. The joints of this set are on the average much thinner and are filled with a powderlike layer of salts, most likely gypsum.

The very high density of fractures indicates a porosity that allows rainwater to seep downward through the joints. This in itself is an important factor in the general setting of the tomb of Nefertari. No one is certain about the cause of deterioration of the wall painting. The possibilities include: (a) rainwater from above; (b) groundwater from below; and (c) humidity from the air inside. If the latter is the main cause, this would speak in favor of closing the tomb to visitors because their presence would significantly increase the humidity inside the tomb. From my preliminary observations, however, it appears likely that the largest amount of moisture reaches the tomb as rainwater seeping through the numerous fractures and joints. Nonetheless, the resolution of this very important point must await conclusions drawn from the hydrological model.

The highly fractured nature of the rock that encloses the tomb of Nefertari suggests that microseismicity can be dangerous in the area. Induced shaking by vehicles and large tourist buses, for example, may dislodge loose pieces of the wall. Further damage may be caused by thixotropy (the property of becoming more fluid when shaken), particularly if water becomes mixed with clays and/or other fine particulate material in the fractures and

Figure 5. Floor plan (top) and cross-section (bottom) of the tomb of Nefertari; 10m deep.

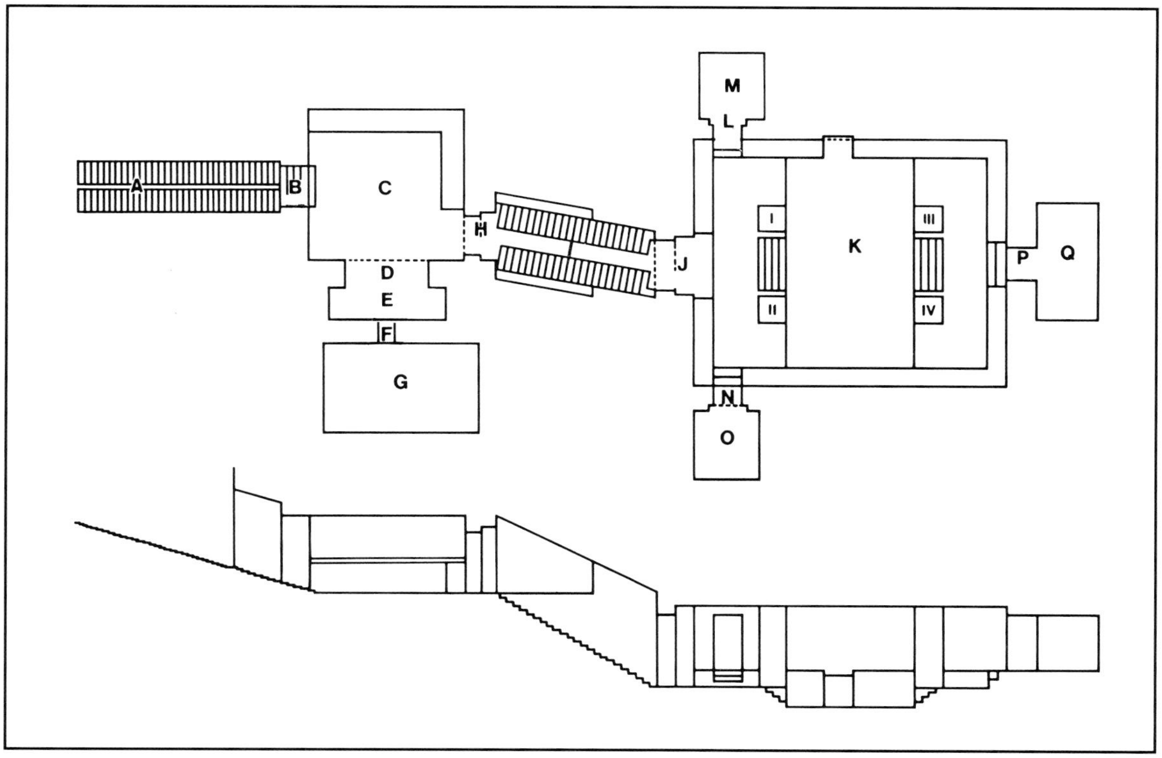

joints. Therefore, it is here recommended that the present paved road that leads to the tomb be shortened by at least 200 m and a new parking lot be established away from the tomb entrance.

For the same reason, disposition of water or any other fluids at or near the surface of the tomb should be prohibited. Any fluids at the surface will eventually make their way to the tomb walls through the fractures and joints in the country rock.

Local structures in the escarpment that trends NE-SW and borders the Valley of the Queens on the north side may play a major role in the structural setting, drainage pattern control, and ultimately the channeling of rainwater to the walls of the tomb. These features, including an open fissure and tilted block, are clearly illustrated in figure 4.

The open fissure is a few meters wide, and from it emanate minute drainage lines that lead to the level of the tomb entrances below. One of these lines runs parallel to the edge of the major rockfall, which forms a deltalike pattern that covers part of the scarp. This fissure and associated features should be studied in detail to establish their effects on the porosity of the rocks in the region and on surface and subsurface drawings.

The tilted block bounds the region of the tombs on the south side (figure 4). The considerable degree of tilt indicates a major event that must have affected the microtectonics of the region. Thus, this block should also be studied in detail to establish its effects on the region.

To establish the particular setting of the tomb of Nefertari, two tombs—one on either side—were visited for comparison. It was immediately noticed that both tombs are at higher levels than that of Nefertari and that their wall paintings and plaster layer are not as badly affected by the same processes that have caused deterioration in the tomb of Nefertari.

The shallower tomb is on the right side of Nefertari's. It is assigned number 68 and belongs to Queen Merit-Amon, who is believed to have been the daughter of Rameses II. On entering this tomb one is struck by the ordered nature of the joint systems in the clayey limestone rock. The rhomboidal fracture pattern is particularly pronounced in the ceilings of the entrance hall and two chambers on either side. The tomb has been inhabited in recent times, and parts of its walls and most of its ceilings are covered by a thick layer of soot from cooking fires. The joints in this tomb are usually thin (a few millimeters wide) and contain gypsum. Tasting of the gypsum filling indicates the lack of rock salt (NaCl). This is true even when the joints are only hair thin.

The tomb to the left of Nefertari's is deeper than number 68 by a few meters and is similar in its fracture pattern. Its limestone appears to be more clayey, however, and its concoidal fracture is not as obvious as in the shallower tomb. The ceilings in this tomb are comparatively high, which hampers observation of their texture. They appear to be even higher than the ceilings of the tomb of Nefertari.

The joints in the deeper tomb appear to be more closely spaced and contain just as much gypsum as in the shallower tomb. A most interesting observation, established by tasting, is the presence of minute amounts of rock salt mixed in with the gypsum that fills the joints.

Cursory comparison of the three tombs suggests a distinct stratigraphic layering in this section of the limestone in the Valley of the Queens. It appears that in the uppermost horizon the limestone is denser and the joints are more widely spaced. The deeper the horizon, the more irregular and, in most cases, more closely spaced the jointing pattern becomes.

The most significant change with depth appears to be the increase in the NaCl content in the gypsum filling the joints and fissures in the rock. Preliminary examination of the plaster in these tombs indicates that its deterioration increases with depth; it is least affected in the shallowest tomb and most deteriorated in the deepest burial chamber of the Nefertari tomb. This condition strongly suggests a correlation between the presence of rock salt and deterioration of the plaster along the walls of the tomb of Nefertari.

It is perhaps significant to note that there are several degrees of deterioration in the tomb of Nefertari. On entering the tomb one immediately notices the vast network of minute fractures in the ceiling, which is painted blue, a color that is believed to be "synthetic" (Jaksch, et al. 1983). This fracturing is unlike any elsewhere in the tomb and is not duplicated in the ceiling of the lower burial chamber.

The second—and unique—deterioration is that which accompanies the dark green color in the wall paintings. This is most noticeable in the figure of the goddess Hat-hur painted in the stairway that leads from the upper to the lower chamber. This particular deterioration appears to affect a paper-thin layer and may be related to the paint or its binding medium. Therefore, it may be one case in which moisture in the air may be playing a role in deterioration.

The third and most damaging type of deterioration is related to the crystallization of rock salt. This takes several forms. The most common is where salt crystallized along the line that separates the plaster layer from the rock. In most cases this induces buckling of the plaster layer with its paint layer until it cracks and falls off. In some cases this causes a segment of plaster, usually a few centimeters in diameter, to separate from the wall and protrude on a pedestal of rock salt crystals.

A further type of salt crystallization is what appears as pustules on the outer surface of the paint layer. This is particularly visible in the side chamber to the right of the burial chamber. This type may also be related to the humidity inside the tomb. Therefore, examination of the microclimate inside the tomb chambers would be significant in establishing such relationships.

The observations here discussed were made during a few days of site inspection and must not be considered conclusive. These observations, however, point to the need of several courses of study that may shed more light on the geographic and geologic setting of the tomb of Nefertari. A full understanding of this setting is essential to the planning of any consolidation and treatment, temporary as well as permanent, of the wall paintings of the tomb.

References

El-Baz, F. 1979. *Egypt as Seen by Landsat*. Cairo.

El-Etr, H. A., A. R. Moustafa, and F. El-Baz. 1979. "Photolineaments in the ASTP stereostrip of the Western Desert of Egypt." *Apollo-Soyuz Test Project Summary Science Report*. Vol. 2 *Earth Observation and Photography*, F. El-Baz and D.M. Warner, eds., NASA SP-412: 97-105.

Esmael, F.A. 1986. *The Tomb of Queen Nefertari: An Overview*. Preliminary Report to the Egyptian Antiquities Organization—The Getty Conservation Institute Joint Working Group.

Jaksch, H. et al. 1983. "Egyptian blue—cuprorivaite: window to ancient Egyptian technology." *Naturwissenschaften* 70, No. 11: 525-35.

Weeks, K.R. 1981. *The Berkeley Map of the Theban Necropolis: Report of the Fourth Season*.

Yehia, M. A. 1973. "Some aspects of the structural geology and stratigraphy of selected parts of the Nile Basin of Upper Egypt." Ph.D. dis., Ain Shams University, Cairo.

Biological Investigations

Hideo Arai

First, a general biological survey was undertaken in the tomb of Nefertari. It was discovered that the tomb has a surprisingly dry environment, with a relative humidity between 30 and 40%. Several spiders were found at the top corner of the east wall in the east side room O. This wall may be the wettest part in the tomb. A silverfish was found in inner room Q, indicating the presence of a starchy substance on which the silverfish could feed and a moderate amount of water. Rodent feces were found on the west side of corridor I. Many ecdyses of dermestid beetles were collected on the floor of the northwest wall of outer hall C.

Although the tomb ceiling was painted Egyptian blue, the color has turned black in the ceiling of west side room M and east side room O. The discoloration may be caused by microorganisms. Fine cracks appear on the surface of the blue paint layers. Paint layers have detached from the rock, and sections of the ceiling have been lost. Salt crystallization was observed on the ceiling of west side room M, east side room O, and inner room Q. Microbiological investigations in the tomb were performed on 8 and 11 September 1986. Air-borne microorganisms in the tomb were measured before and after the investigations by project members.

Measuring points in the tomb were fixed at outer hall C, sarcophagus chamber K, inner room Q, and in the open air (see table 1). The method of obtaining microbial counts was as follows: one end of a silicon tube was fixed at the center of each room, the other end was connected to the slit of a pinhole air sampler. Then air, at the rate of 26.5 liters per minute, was blown by a compressor onto three kinds of sterilized plate media through the pinholes of the air sampler for two minutes. After these plate media were incubated for seven days at 25° C, colonies of microorganisms on the media were counted. Measurements of air-borne microorganisms outside the tomb were also compared.

The number of filamentous microorganisms (fungi) per cubic meter found in the tomb was 141 at outer hall C, 104 at sarcophagus chamber K, and 66 at inner room Q, while the number of nonfilamentous microorganisms (mainly bacteria) was 2,800; 3,185; and 2,722; respectively. The counts of fungi and bacteria in the tomb were of a uniform number

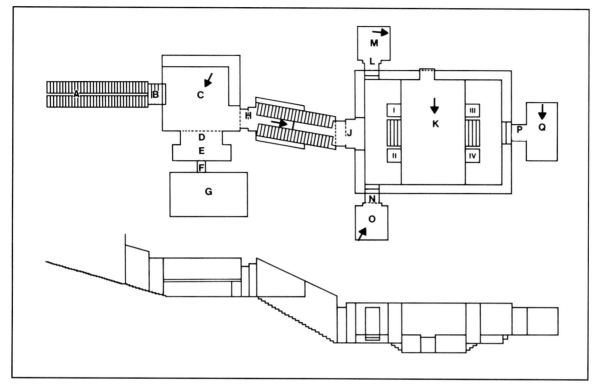

Figure 1. Plan and cross-section of Nefertari's tomb showing locations where biological measurements were made.

at every point. The number of fungi and bacteria in inner room Q was the lowest. At the same time the number of fungi and bacteria per cubic meter in the open air was 804 and 2,192.

Microbial counts per cubic meter on the morning of 11 September 1986 were 365 at outer hall C and 237 at sarcophagus chamber K for fungi, while those for bacteria were 5,576 at outer hall C and 5,557 at sarcophagus chamber K. Therefore, the numbers of fungi and bacteria in the tomb after investigations doubled in comparison with the number before the investigations. The numbers of microorganisms per cubic meter in the open air at the same time were 567 for fungi and 2,174 for bacteria.

The humidity in the tomb was very low, perhaps below 50% RH. Accumulated micropowder from walls and rocks, which had settled on the floor, was agitated by any movement within the tomb, thereby influencing the microbial counts. The large number of bacteria and fungi per cubic meter, 2,700-3,200 and 66-141, is a result of movements made during investigations. The microbial counts per cubic meter made after the investigations were about 5,500. This number is rather low compared with the number counted before the investigations. By the time the microorganisms had been measured, some fifteen hours after the investigations, large micropowder particles, which had earlier been disturbed by

DATE	MICROORGANISM	SAMPLING POINTS			
		Outer Hall C	Sarcophagus Chamber K	Inner-Room Q	Open Air
September 8, 1986 (before investigations)	Non-filamentous microorganisms	2800	3185	2722	2192
	Filamentous microorganisms	141	104	66	804
	Rate of Cladosporium (%)	0	---	---	39
September 11, 1986 (after investigations)	Non-filamentous microorganisms	5576	5557	---	2174
	Filamentous microorganisms	369	237	---	567
	Rate of Cladosporium (%)	64	72	---	77

Table 1. Numbers of microorganisms before and after investigation in the tomb of Nefertari (Number/m³).

movement within the tomb, had already settled on the floor.

The most marked change observed in the airborne microorganisms of the tomb was the change in number of Cladosporium spp. Although Cladosporium spp. were not found in the microbial counts before the investigations, they increased 64-72% in fungi after the investigations. In measurements in the open air 40-77% of fungi were found to be Cladosporium spp. The circulation of fresh air in and outside the tomb was extremely restricted. Therefore, the existence of Cladosporium spp. demonstrates an exchange of ventilation outside and inside the tomb.

The fungi Acremonium sp., Actinomycetes Aspergillus spp., Emericella sp., and Penicillium spp. were isolated from the tomb, while Aspergillus spp., Emericella sp., Epicoccum sp., and Penicillium spp. were isolated from the open air. The bacteria Bacillus spp. and Micrococcus spp. were mainly isolated, and Bacillus spp. were the dominant genus in the tomb.

The small black parts of west side room M were incubated at Aw 0.94, 24°C for more than three months to test whether the discoloration was caused by fungi. After making the fungi grow, mycological experiments were begun and are now being performed.

At the entrance of the tomb is an iron door, with many netted holes about 5 cm wide, which may influence ventilation. What appear to be rodent and spider paths have been found near the tomb entrance.

Salt crystallizations about 3-4 cm deep have formed on the northwest wall of sarcophagus chamber K. As a result pieces of wall painting have been pushed forward about 3-4 cm from their original position.

Several spiders were found at the corner of the ceiling of the east wall in east side room O. Comparatively large salt crystallizations were also recognized on the ceiling of

Figure 2. Airborne microorganisms were measured inside the tomb and in the open air.

what is considered to be the wettest part of the tomb. It is recommended that water activity in the tomb be maintained in a state of equilibrium with, or higher than, that of the mother rock of the wall paintings to stop the crystallization under the wall paintings. This will require re-creating of the environment before the tomb was first excavated.

When the tomb was discovered in 1904 the wall paintings had been preserved in a stable condition for more than three thousand years. Investigation of the environment of other unexcavated tombs or long reburied tombs in Luxor should be made to identify the best burial condition. When such an investigation is made, it will be possible to maintain the excavated tombs of Nefertari in a stable condition.

Microflora Investigations

Mokhtar S. Ammar
Kamal Barakat
Esam H. Ghanem
Asmaa A. El-Deeb

Seven samples were isolated from the tomb of Nefertari, which include four samples from the walls, two samples from the air, and one sample from the ceiling of the tomb. The samples were taken from specific locations:

1. A swab from the right wall at the entrance of the tomb (see plan of the tomb, location 1, wall 4, room B), where there are scattered soft-black and gray spots among relatively wide areas on the wall paintings.

2. A swab from one of the walls of room H where there are many black spots. The effect of humidity and the presence of many salts on both walls and ceiling of room H (location 2) could be readily detected.

3. A swab from the left corner of room H (location 3), where there are many scattered black spots.

4. A swab from a salt location on one of the walls of room G (location 4), where there are many salt crystals in the form of white needles, which fall constantly from the walls and ceiling of the room.

5. An atmospheric air sample taken outside the entrance of room H after being exposed for ten minutes outside room H, next to wall 6 of room E (location 5).

6. An atmospheric air sample from room H (location 6).

7. A salt sample from the ceiling of room G (location 7).

The isolated microorganisms belong to three different microbial groups: bacteria (thirty isolates), yeasts (three isolates), and fungi (one isolate). The bacteria isolates were identified to the genus level in the following groups:

1. Includes gram-negative isolates of two genera: genus *Alcaligenes*, which includes four isolates symbolized as N1, N4, N6, and N13 (see photomicrographs) and genus *Acinetobacter*, which includes two isolates, N7 and N8 (see photomicrographs).

2. Includes gram-positive sporing rods of the genus *Bacillus*. This group includes twelve isolates symbolized as N2, N3, N5, N11, N14, N16, N17, N20, N24, N26, N26, and N28 (see photomicrographs).

3. Includes gram-positive cocci. This group includes six isolates of the genus *Micrococcus*, symbolized as N9, N11, N13, N18, N25, and N27 (see photomicrographs).

4. Includes gram-positive nonsporing irregular forms. These include three genera: genus *Listeria* (one isolate [N13a]), genus *Corynebacterium* (one isolate [N15]), genus *Arthrobacter* (three isolates [N19, N22, N23]).

Only three isolates of unicellular yeasts were found to follow the genus *Rhodosporidium*; these were symbolized as N12, NY1, and NY2 (see photomicrographs). Only one isolate of filamentous fungi seems to be unique in its morphology. It belongs to the genus *Penicillium*.

The isolated microbial strains comprise three groups of microbes: bacteria (thirty

Figure 1. Plan of the tomb showing locations where samples were taken.

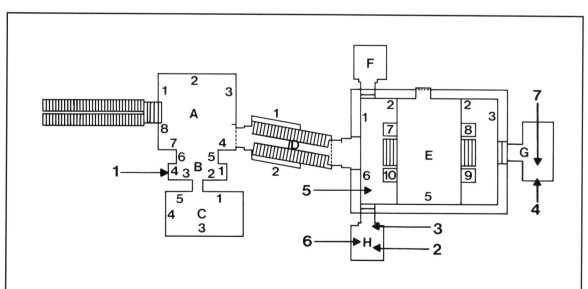

strains), yeasts (three strains), fungi (one strain). The isolated microbial groups represent the microflora of the walls, air, and ceiling of the tomb of Nefertari. Identification of all referenced isolates to the species level will be carried out in further work. Phase-contrast photomicrographs of all the isolated microbes under investigation, except the genus *Penicillium*, have been taken. Electron photomicrographs will be obtained for those strains that exhibit special biochemical and/or physiological activities and appear to play a major role in the process of biodeterioration inside the Nefertari and other tombs.

The investigations of the present work found many black spots and biodeteriorated places on the walls and ceiling of the tomb. This deterioration is shown by the presence of crystalline salt materials and loss of binding property in the wall paintings. It is planned to identify the relation between the isolated microbes in the present work and any biodeteriorations occurring on the painted walls. For this reason the isolated microbes (bacteria, yeast, and fungi) will be subject to a special microbiological and/or biochemical study. The work will be planned as follows:

1. The biochemical role of each isolated strain concerning the biodeterioration process occurring on the ceiling and walls of the tomb will be studied.

2. Since we have investigated the microbial flora of the tomb of Tut-Ankh Amen and because there is a great similarity between the infection occurring in both tombs, it is believed that there is a common factor in the biodeterioration in both. If the microbe is the common factor responsible for biodeterioration, the following steps must be taken: (1) search for the origin of contamination. This task requires the cooperation of the Egyptian Antiquities Organization staff to provide historical and archaeological data; (2) study the mechanism inhibiting the growth of each isolated microbial strain, without affecting the walls, paintings and decorations, or ceiling; (3) Study the biochemical and/or physiological relation of microbial growth to the following: (*a*) the introduced pigments in the decorative paints and drawings; (*b*) the colors and binding materials such as gypsum, resins, albumins, beeswax, gums, clay, glue, salts, starches, and asphalt; (*c*) any other minute quantities of materials from pictures and works of art.

Also, by examining the tomb we found:

1. Several dead bodies of small spiders that frequently live in areas such as this one and cause no direct damage to the wall.

2. Insect infestation with the silverfish *Thermobia aegyptica* (Thysanura) in almost all chambers of the tomb but mainly in the first hall where it moves rapidly over the walls and hides in the cracks.

    Usually we find this insect in the museum libraries. It attacks paper, bookbindings, and glue. Sometimes it feeds on dry plants and fine old textiles, especially if they are starched. We believe that this insect was introduced into the tomb with straw,

Figure 2.   Photomicrographs of Group 1 and Group 2 bacteria.

PHOTOMICROGRAPHS OF GROUP 1 BACTERIA

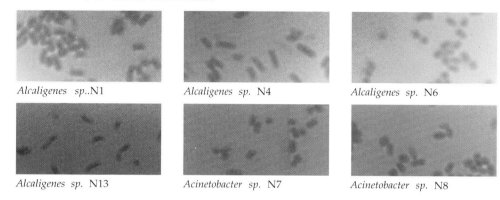

Alcaligenes sp..N1   *Alcaligenes sp. N4*   *Alcaligenes sp. N6*

Alcaligenes sp. N13   *Acinetobacter sp. N7*   *Acinetobacter sp. N8*

PHOTOMICROGRAPHS OF GROUP 2 BACTERIA

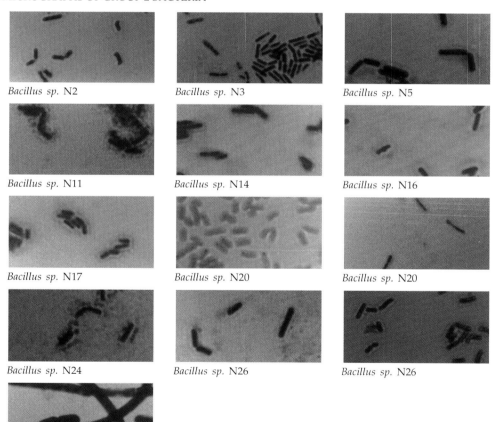

Bacillus sp. N2   *Bacillus sp. N3*   *Bacillus sp. N5*

Bacillus sp. N11   *Bacillus sp. N14*   *Bacillus sp. N16*

Bacillus sp. N17   *Bacillus sp. N20*   *Bacillus sp. N20*

Bacillus sp. N24   *Bacillus sp. N26*   *Bacillus sp. N26*

Bacillus sp. N28

Figure 3. Photomicrographs of Group 3 and Group 4 bacteria and yeasts.

PHOTOMICROGRAPHS OF GROUP 3 BACTERIA

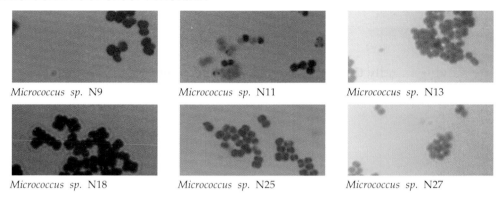

Micrococcus sp. N9   *Micrococcus sp.* N11   *Micrococcus sp.* N13

Micrococcus sp. N18   *Micrococcus sp.* N25   *Micrococcus sp.* N27

PHOTOMICROGRAPHS OF GROUP 4 BACTERIA

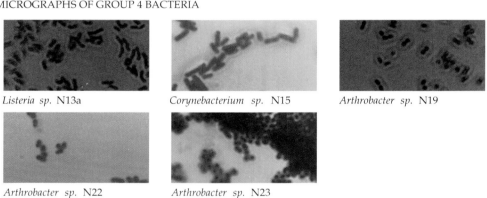

Listeria sp. N13a   *Corynebacterium sp.* N15   *Arthrobacter sp.* N19

Arthrobacter sp. N22   *Arthrobacter sp.* N23

PHASE CONTRAST PHOTOMICROGRAPHS OF YEASTS

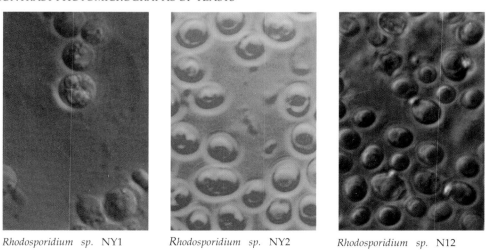

Rhodosporidium sp. NY1   *Rhodosporidium sp.* NY2   *Rhodosporidium sp.* N12

paper, or cartons used to encase materials and equipment.

Damage:

1. If the surface layer contains a chopped straw, the insect will feed upon it and weaken the layer.

2. By moving rapidly through the cracks and between the surface layer and original wall of the tomb, the insect causes the same result that facilitates the detachment of this layer.

Treatment:

1. Gammexan candeps. This fumigant kills insects at once; it is capable of penetrating through holes and cracks, and gives good results. However, a light yellowish precipitate may form over the surfaces; this can be easily removed by brushing.

2. Carbon disulphide. A liquid that evaporates in almost four hours; also gives very good results and has no side effects. We used it in enclosed spaces.

Microclimatic Conditions

Feisal A. Esmael

Although numerous scientific missions have long frequented the tomb of Nefertari, they have succeeded only in creating tidal waves of alternating hope and despair. The tomb's awesome physical conditions and complex nature have established the microclimate as the controlling factor in the extent and variety of misfortunes that have befallen that remarkable monument. Thus, the assessment of the microenvironment may be one clue to identifying the origin of resident problems and the key to possible future answers.

Two thermodynamic parameters, temperature and relative humidity (RH), are particularly crucial to any assessment, and initial investigations were limited to a few spot readings of these parameters, which were noted at arbitrary locations inside the tomb and were intuitively taken as representative of the whole. Systematic recordings and specific measurements eventually followed, with varying degrees of interest and vision. The objective of the present microclimatic survey is the formulation of a thermodynamic model of the tomb.

The earliest records available are of readings taken between 3-5 March 1958 at unspecified locations inside and outside the tomb. The measurements, taken in the mornings (no time stated), give an average temperature of 26.6°C inside, while the temperature outside varied between 20°C and 27°C. Relative humidity inside varied between 27 and 35% while varying outside between 32 and 43%. On 15-16 October 1958 the average values given are 29°C and 26°C and 28% and 43% for temperatures and RH inside and outside the tomb, respectively.

On 4-5 January 1970, however, the individual values given are 27°C, 19°C; 35%, 50%; and 28°C, 25°C; 42%, 57%.

Systematic recording of microclimatic conditions inside the tomb was conducted by a Canadian group from the Chemistry Department of Toronto University during a full week in December 1977. With their inner instrument placed inside the antechamber on the eastern side of the burial hall and the outer instrument placed on the left immediately outside the entrance door, the average values given are 27 ± 1°C for temperature inside and

13-17° C for temperatures outside and 31 ± 2% for RH inside and 50-69% for RH outside. The same group, placing a special recording instrument at the inner location from February to August 1981, reported the following averages: 28.3 ± 0.5°C for temperature inside and between 14.9 ± 1% and 29.3 ± 1% for RH outside.

Microclimatic measurements carried out by the author at different locations inside and outside the tomb during 1983 were the first to cover the whole tomb, with the selection of specific locations suitably distributed (figure 1).

In January 1983, measurements yielded the following averages for the period 12-17 January:

> 14.1 ± 17.3°C and 39-65% RH at location I (outside)
> 24.1 ± 26.6°C and 27-40% RH at location II
> 27.6 ± 0.4°C and 27 ± 2% RH at location III,
> 28.0 ± 0.5°C and 26 ± 2% RH at location IV
> 28.2 ± 0.4°C and 25 ± 3% RH at location V

For the period 8-14 February 1983, measurements yielded the following averages:

> 18.5 - 21°C and 30-39% RH at location I
> 27.2 ± 0.2°C and 24 ± 3% RH at location II
> 28.1 ± 0.1°C and 24 ± 2% RH at location III
> 28.2 ± 0.2°C and 24 ± 3% RH at location IV
> 28.4 ± 0.2°C and 24 ± 2% RH at location V
> 28.5°C and 24 ± 2% RH at location VI
> 27.5°C and 24 ± 2% RH at location VII

On 23 March 1983, a large joint team (the Egyptian Antiquities Organization and SWECO) stayed inside the tomb for two hours (0900-1100) and measurements taken before and after the visit yielded the following averages:

> 21 ± 1.2°C and 29 ± 4% RH at location I
> 27.1 ± 0.1°C and 29 ± 1% RH at location II
> 28.3 ± 0.3°C and 28% RH at location III
> 28.3 ± 0.2°C and 27 ± 1% RH at location IV
> 28.6°C and 28% RH at location V
> 28.4 ± 0.2°C and 28% RH at location VI
> 27.5°C and 29 ± 2% RH at location VII

For 8-9 September 1983, moreover, the average results at the selected locations were:

> 33 ± 3°C and 22-40% RH at location I
> 29.3 ± 0.3°C and 40 ± 2% RH at location II
> 29.3 ± 0.3°C and 38 ± 1% RH at location III

29.3 ± 0.3°C and 39 ± 2% RH at location IV
29.3 ± 0.3°C and 41 ± 2% RH at location V
29.3 ± 0.3°C and 41 ± 2% RH at location VI
29.3 ± 0.3°C and 39 ± 2% RH at location VII

Finally measurements during the period 1-5 October 1983 yielded the following averages for the selected locations (I, II, III, IV, V, VI, and VII), respectively:

26 - 33°C and 25-40% RH at location I
29.2 ± 0.2°C and 35% RH at location II
29°C and 35 ± 1% RH at location III
29.1 ± 0.1°C and 35 ± 1% RH at location IV
29.3 ± 0.1°C and 36 ± 1% RH at location V
29.1 ± 0.1°C and 35 ± 1% RH at location VI
29.2 ± 0.2°C and 35 ± 1% RH at location VII

Commencing on 18 September 1986, we conducted the systematic recording of temperature and relative humidity inside the tomb, taking the climatological normals for the Luxor area (available for the last sixty years) as representative of the prevailing conditions outside the tomb. The investigation was designed to conclude after one year, but is now expected to be extended for routine microclimatic monitoring during subsequent conservation campaigns.

Figure 1. Locations of spot measurements during the 1983 campaign.

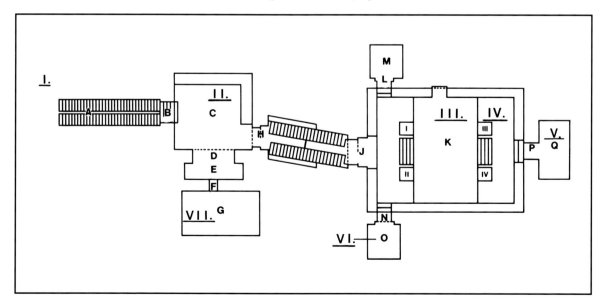

One data logger and two identical temperature-relative humidity recorders were employed. The former was assumed to have a running capacity of three months with monthly power supply servicing, but was later found to require a constant electric supply, which could not be safely provided in the tomb. The other recording instruments performed fairly well.

The pair of operating chart-recording instruments, with a running capacity of up to thirty-three days each, were moved to ten different locations inside the tomb (see figure 2). Entry to the tomb was fully documented, with the number of visitors and duration of visits recorded. This latter step was deemed necessary to assess the influence of human presence on the microenvironment of the tomb and to establish the conditions under which future conservation work may proceed without adversely disturbing the microclimatic conditions inside.

The current microclimatic survey has yielded the following averages:

30.2 $\pm$ 0.2% RH at location 1 (figure 2),
30.1 $\pm$ 0.1°C and 32 $\pm$ 2% RH at location 2
during the period 18 September to 19 October 1986;

30.0 $\pm$ 0.5°C and 26 $\pm$ 4% RH at location 3,
30.0 $\pm$ 0.5°C and 28 $\pm$ 3% RH at location 4
during the period 22 October to 24 November 1986;

Figure 2. Locations of recording instruments during the period 18 September 1986-15 March 1987.

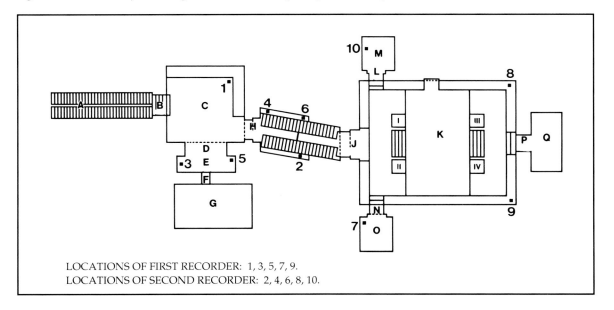

LOCATIONS OF FIRST RECORDER: 1, 3, 5, 7, 9.
LOCATIONS OF SECOND RECORDER: 2, 4, 6, 8, 10.

29°C and 22 $\pm$ 1% RH at location 5,
29.5°C and 22 $\pm$ 2% RH at location 6
during the period 3 December 1986 to 4 January 1987;

29.3 $\pm$ 0.3°C and 20 $\pm$ 3% RH at location 7,
29.3 $\pm$ 0.3°C and 20 $\pm$ 2% RH at location 8
during the period 8 January to 8 February 1987.

Locations 9, 10 (figure 2) indicate the present positions of the two instruments.

Summary

The systematic work described in the preceding two sections has the added advantage of being carried out by one individual (the author), securing a reasonable degree of continuity, homogeneity, and consistency. The applied procedures were been well-defined throughout and it has, therefore, been safe to assume that the amassed data may be treated with justified confidence, allowing one to draw the basic conclusions through which future conservation campaigns can be conceived. The conclusions are summarized as follows:

1. Human presence in the tomb during the period 18 September 1986 - 12 February 1987 amounts to about four hundred hours. On occasions as many as twenty-five individuals were present in the tomb at one time. No significant microclimatic changes could, however, be detected in association with any of those frequent and sometimes massive entries.

2. The microclimate of the tomb appears to undergo detectable seasonable variations.

3. Temperature values fluctuate between 26 and 30° C, and RH between about 20 and 45%.

4. Within one season temperature is practically steady and relative humidity thus becomes the one critical climatic factor.

5. Conservation treatment is intended to proceed with the utmost care and extreme caution. Limits, therefore, may be imposed on the number of persons working inside the tomb at one time. Selecting the driest period of the year (inside the tomb) would also be imperative.

6. Gentle ventilation and marginal cooling could be applied, if absolutely necessary, for workers' comfort and greater efficiency.

7. While constant monitoring of the microclimate is not absolutely essential within the imposed limits on human presence, it shall still remain advisable.

Color Measurements

Frank Preusser
Michael Schilling

The purpose of making color measurements in the tomb of Nefertari is to accurately record the colors found in various wall paintings before conservation treatment is begun. Selected measurement locations represent the various states of preservation found in the tomb, ranging from well-preserved areas to areas of near-total deterioration with loose painted-plaster fragments. A modified Minolta CR-121 ChromaMeter with a DP-100 data processor was used to measure the samples. Measurements were made on every color occurring in each of the seven paintings examined. Photographs documenting the locations of the measurements were taken; these locations are cross-referenced to the plan of the tomb. Samples of painted and unpainted plaster were also taken from storage boxes in the tomb as well as samples of salt crystallization from the plaster surfaces. Additionally Feisal A. Esmael selected two salt samples for testing by the Getty Conservation Institute. For continuous recording of humidity and temperature, monitoring equipment was installed in various locations in the tomb. The humidity and temperature measurements may be found here in a separate report, "Microclimatic Conditions," by Prof. Esmael.

The Minolta reflectance meter with data processor was chosen for several reasons. It is portable, requires no sampling, allows for multiple calibrations, and provides color-space evaluation in four modes. To make a measurement the measuring head must contact the colored surface. A holder normally ensures that the head is held perpendicular to the sample surface and is very satisfactory for measuring solid, planar surfaces such as color-calibration tiles. Wall paintings, however, are fragile, easily abraded, and have irregular surfaces. Use of the holder is thereby prohibited. Another problem preventing the implementation of the instrument in the tomb is that the measuring head is metal and capable of damaging the surface on contact. These difficulties had to be overcome before making measurements in the tomb.

      The CR-121 is designed to operate with or without the holder, the use of which merely ensures that the measuring head is maintained perpendicular to the surface. The end of the measuring head is flat; positioning may also be accomplished easily without the holder. Improper positioning of the head changes the values of the measurement since the geometry is disturbed. Therefore, measurements were made on color-tile standards with and without the holder to verify the reproducibility of the positioning of the measuring head. Reproducibility can be expressed by the standard deviations of both sets of data. The error in reproducing the position of the measuring head was estimated to be small when compared with the error introduced by the irregularity of the plaster surfaces.

The addition of a thin white pad to the end of the measuring head prevented the instrument from scratching the plaster. A small hole was cut into a thin strip of Goretek, which was then taped over the end of the measuring head. The hole was cut slightly larger than the interior diameter of the measuring head to prevent overlapping of the Goretek with the hole. A thin piece was used to minimize changes in the measuring geometry. Any changes that would occur would be compensated for by the calibration procedures.

Evaluation of the modification and calibration of the equipment was carried out systematically in the following manner:

1. The unit was calibrated using the holder, without the Goretek padding, on the white Minolta calibration tile, then the color-tile standards were measured. The unit was used with standard illuminant C, and the Y x y system was used to express the data. The known Y x y values were compared to those determined by the instrument (manufacturer's data for the standards are given in table 1).

2. The white, red, green, and cyan tiles were calibrated using the holder, without the Goretek padding, to provide closer reference points. All twelve tiles were then reanalyzed to obtain the optimum determination of Y x y values for this unit. The tile closest in color to the tile to be analyzed was chosen as standard. For example, the red tile was chosen as the reference for the pink, the cyan for the deep blue. All measurements indicate which tile was chosen as standard.

3. The holder was then removed, and the twelve tiles were reanalyzed using the calibration data from step 2. The Y x y values were then compared to those from step 2, and the differences indicate the error associated with manually holding the head perpendicular to the surface.

4. The Goretek padding was added, and the twelve tiles were remeasured. The data were compared to the results from steps 2-3 to determine the error introduced by the Goretek, due in part to changes in geometry and the difficulty in maintaining the head perpendicular to the surface.

5. Finally the padded unit, without the holder, was calibrated on the white, red, green, and cyan tiles. All twelve tiles were then reanalyzed. This was the final configuration of the instrument, and these calibrations would be used when making measurements in the tomb.

The data from the step-by-step calibration indicated that the removal of the holder and addition of the Goretek had little effect on the measurements and the modified unit should be satisfactory for making the measurements.

Table 1. *Manufacturer's data for the standards. Luminance and chromaticity values for illuminant C/2° observer.*

0°/45° geometry

	Y	x	y
Pale gray	60.5	0.310	0.317
Midgray	24.0	0.310	0.317
Difference gray	24.1	0.312	0.326
Deep gray	4.7	0.312	0.320
Deep pink	11.5	0.407	0.295
Red	8.5	0.615	0.325
Orange	35.3	0.530	0.395
Bright yellow	64.5	0.455	0.485
Green	19.3	0.275	0.415
Difference green	19.6	0.283	0.428
Cyan	17.8	0.195	0.225
Deep blue	1.0	0.185	0.097

Ceramic Color Standards supplied by the British Ceramic Research Association Ltd.

Measurement Locations

The paintings in the tomb are in various states of preservation, depending primarily on location. The type of conservation treatment a painting will receive is chosen in part by its state of preservation. Because each type of conservation treatment may affect the paint layers differently, it was decided to make color measurements on paintings in various states of preservation. The individual paintings were selected by severity of damage and ease of accessibility, and all colors representing the palette in each area were measured. Seven paintings were examined.

The locations of the paintings are indicated on the plan of the tomb (figure 1). Each room or area is given a letter, then paintings photographed in a single room are numbered consecutively. For example, the plan shows that eight areas were photographed in sarcophagus chamber K. Many photographs were taken to document the state of preservation of the tomb in addition to those taken of the areas where colors were measured.

Areas selected for color measurements were photographed in the following manner: first an overall picture was taken to document the composition and its location. Then, close-ups were made to record the precise locations of the measured areas. Close-ups were designated with letters, such as A and B. Photographs of the measured areas accompany this report.

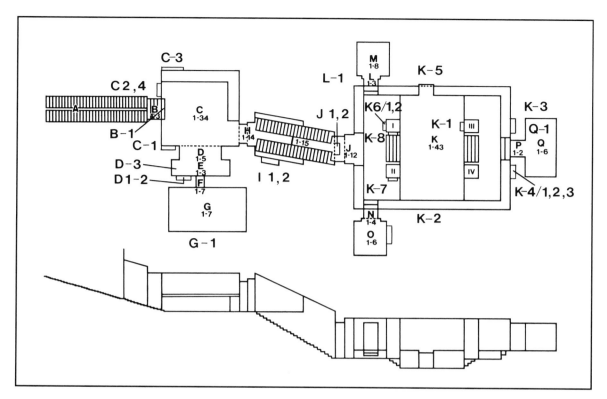

Figure 1. Plan and cross-section of Nefertari's tomb showing locations of technical photographs for color measurements.

Procedures

Every effort was made to select areas of original color, avoiding overpaintings and restorations. After the seven compositions for measurement were selected each was examined under incandescent light to find places representing the individual colors of the composition. After preliminary selections were made these areas were further examined under a 350 nm ultraviolet light source. Restorations fluoresce more intensely under ultraviolet light and can be easily differentiated from original paint layers. The final locations where readings were to be made were marked on a Polaroid photograph of the area.

The locations to be measured were lightly dusted with a soft squirrel-hair brush while air was blown from a bulb syringe over the surface to remove surface contamination. Because of the inhomogeneity of the colored areas, three measurement locations were selected for each color occurring in each of the seven paintings. The range of Y x y values found for each color is related to the homogeneity for that color and surface roughness.

To determine the reproducibility of the entire measuring scheme one composition (D-1) was completely measured twice. This procedure tested the precision of the photograph marking and subsequent relocation to make measurements and the reproducibility of positioning the measuring head.

When the measurements were made the measuring head touched the wall with very slight pressure to avoid damaging the surface. Because the surfaces are not totally flat a completely light-tight seal could not be achieved in each measurement. This problem most affects the Y value of the measurement since Y is related to brightness.

Results

Table 2 lists the results of the reproducibility study performed on location D-1A. Table 3 lists the color measurements of location K-1A. The color measurement data for the areas is not listed here but is available from the Egyptian Antiquities Organization or the Getty Conservation Institute. The largest differences between the two sets of data are found for the Y values, probably because of surface roughness, since it is difficult to accurately reposition the measuring head on an irregular surface. Statistical evaluation of these data will provide the detection limit for this instrument when used in the tomb. These results will appear in a later report. Munsell color coordinates can be calculated from these numbers to provide a visual indication of the color found at each point. The Munsell data will follow later.

Table 2. Duplicate color measurements of location D-1A.

Color	Standard	Area	Y_1	Y_2	x_1	x_2	y_1	y_2
Gold (flesh)	Green	1	28.8	30.6	0.431	0.430	0.425	0.427
Gold	Green	2	31.9	30.7	0.419	0.430	0.417	0.424
Gold	Green	3	31.1	33.4	0.414	0.408	0.412	0.419
White	White	1	56.4	61.5	0.327	0.329	0.335	0.333
White	White	2	60.5	58.6	0.329	0.330	0.334	0.335
White	White	3	59.3	62.9	0.332	0.328	0.336	0.333
Plaster	White	1	56.0	53.7	0.329	0.331	0.332	0.334
Plaster	White	2	52.2	55.4	0.331	0.330	0.334	0.334
Plaster	White	3	51.0	52.2	0.330	0.331	0.333	0.334
Green	Green	1	26.8	25.4	0.303	0.304	0.354	0.354
Green	Green	2	26.4	25.1	0.308	0.306	0.357	0.355
Green	Green	3	21.7	21.2	0.313	0.317	0.366	0.368
Blue	Cyan	1	6.5	6.4	0.280	0.278	0.313	0.309
Blue	Cyan	2	7.3	6.6	0.286	0.275	0.315	0.306
Blue	Cyan	3	7.0	6.9	0.275	0.287	0.305	0.317
Red	Red	1	18.4	18.2	0.448	0.456	0.345	0.349
Red	Red	2	16.5	16.1	0.457	0.462	0.346	0.347
Red	Red	3	15.3	16.3	0.452	0.457	0.346	0.349

D-1

D-1A

I-1

I-1A

Figure 2. Areas selected for color measurements were photographed to document the composition, then close-ups were made to record precise locations. The sequence of photographs on this and the following page shows various examples.

76

Figure 2 (continued).

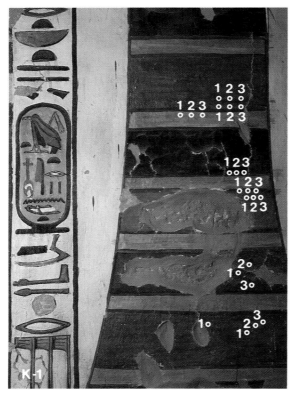

Table 3. Color measurements of location K-1A.

Color	Standard	Area	Y	x	y
Light red	Red	1	18.1	0.487	0.354
Light red	Red	2	18.2	0.485	0.355
Light red	Red	3	18.6	0.471	0.349
Dark red	Red	1	14.0	0.505	0.349
Dark red	Red	2	13.8	0.477	0.343
Dark red	Red	3	11.1	0.487	0.337
Yellow	Green	1	34.0	0.455	0.439
Yellow	Green	2	32.9	0.452	0.438
Yellow	Green	3	34.3	0.451	0.431
Deep blue	Cyan	1	6.3	0.286	0.312
Deep blue	Cyan	2	6.1	0.292	0.315
Deep blue	Cyan	3	6.9	0.281	0.302
Dark red	Red	1	13.0	0.420	0.330
Dark red	Red	2	12.2	0.428	0.332
Dark red	Red	3	11.1	0.433	0.334
Green	Green	1	19.8	0.306	0.374
Green	Green	2	18.8	0.332	0.381
Green	Green	3	19.6	0.303	0.369

References

Billmeyer Jr., Fred W. and Max Saltzman. 1981. *Principles of Color Technology*, Second Edition. New York.

Simon, F. T. and W. J. Goodwin. 1958. "Rapid graphical computation of small color differences, Union Carbide." *American Dyestuff Reporter* 47, p. 105.

Appendix: Status Report on Color Monitoring in the Tomb of Nefertari

This appendix summarizes the current status of the color monitoring program in the tomb of Nefertari. The measuring strategy was modified after a meeting with Max Saltzman, Consultant, Scientific Program, the Getty Conservation Institute.

The calibration procedure has been simplified. The procedure that was originally followed began with calibrating the Minolta CR-121 with data processor on the white tile supplied with the instrument, then further calibrations were performed on three selected color tiles. Deviations from the ideal measuring conditions were determined as the instrument was modified. Contrary to the owner's manual, however, the only proper way to calibrate is on the white tile since the manual does not explain how the instrument is corrected to read properly after calibrating on a colored standard.

The color tiles are useful as reference standards. Measurement of the tiles after calibrating on the white tile (step 1 in original calibration procedure) identifies the overall accuracy of the instrument in measuring the different colors of the tiles. Furthermore, periodic measurement of the tiles can be used to ascertain the stability of the instrument, essential to long-term projects such as this. (For these measurements the assumption is that the tiles are constant.)

Since the initial measurements made in the tomb were based on these earlier calibrations, a correction must be made to correlate them with future measurements. Therefore, during the next measurement campaign, all the original areas tested that have not yet been treated by Paolo Mora will be reanalyzed using the old and new procedures. These data can be compared graphically, using a procedure discussed later in this report to determine the offset produced by the original calibration procedure. Measurements on any areas that have already been treated can be corrected using the offsets found above.

The parameters used to express color, Y x y, are not independent variables but are related to each other in a complex mathematical expression. Repetitive measurements on a single tile should not be averaged and the spread of readings expressed by a standard deviation. The graphical procedure, discussed later, provides a way of estimating the precision of the readings.

The next change in the measuring strategy concerns the presentation of data. The former plan was to convert the data, originally expressed in Y x y coordinates, to Munsell notation. Then, given the data, the color could easily be found in the Munsell book of color. Any changes of the colors in the tomb caused by the conservation treatment could be displayed on the appropriate color chips.

A method has been developed that permits calculation of small color differences and is ideally suited for the present purpose. Chromaticity measurements (in x and y) are plotted on specially prepared uniform chromaticity charts that display chromaticity differences on a uniform basis relative to a ruler scale. Uncorrected chromaticity differences are read from the graph and then are plotted against the lightness value (ΔY) on one of thirteen color-difference calculating charts. Total color difference (ΔA), corrected chromaticity difference (ΔC), and lightness difference (ΔL) are read directly from the graph. All these differences are relative to a control sample. The application of this system to this project is summarized as follows.

First, data from the periodic measurements of the color-reference tiles can be plotted to show if there is any drift in the instrument with time or if random scattering of the data points occurs. Next, the stepwise modification to the instrument can be followed graphically also to determine if the addition of Goretek or the removal of the measuring-head holder has any specific influence on the readings of the color-reference tiles. As an example, the data for the red tile in table 4 was plotted to illustrate the method. The numbers indicate the five steps in the procedure and the graphs show that the largest color difference occurs for the initial reading of the red tile when the instrument was calibrated on the white tile.

The data from the measurements in the tomb can be plotted on these charts also. Replicate measurements made on specific areas in the tomb provide information concerning the precision of the measurements (determined by the spread of the data points found from each graph). Then, as the measurements are made throughout the tomb, the first reading taken at each location is considered the control sample, mentioned earlier. The precision of the measurements is used to mark out a control region from which differences are calculated. An example was prepared using data from the red areas in location D-1A listed in table 2. The length of the lines connecting the points on the chromaticity diagram show the reproducibility of the two measurements (a and b), which were made at three red areas. The longest line represents approximately four units of uncorrected chromaticity difference between point 'a' (the control sample) and 'b' (the reading). (When measured in 1/2-inch increments, the length of the lines reads out directly in difference units.)

Looking at the color difference charts, one triangle has been marked to show the relationship between A, L, and C. It is seen that the largest A occurs for area 3 and is approximately four units. This means that the precision of the measurements (considering these data only) is no better than four units. This chart also can be used to show changes in relative lightness (ΔL). Area 3 shows an increase in L compared with the control. Shifts in L can be used to determine if lightening or darkening of a location is occurring (if the shift is outside of the range of measuring error, which is not the case for the example).

The last point to be discussed concerns the Munsell book of colors. Measurements can be made on selected color chips and these data plotted. The relationship can be found between the number of color difference units on adjacent chips for the colors measured. Then the difference data can also be expressed as a certain number or fraction of Munsell chips. This provides a good visual indication since the Munsell system is based on visual differences.

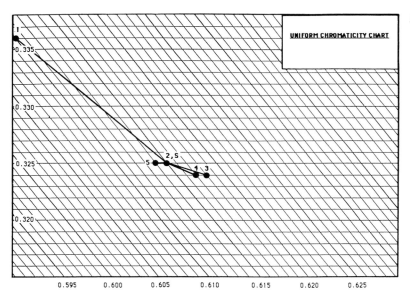

Figure 3. Red reference tile.

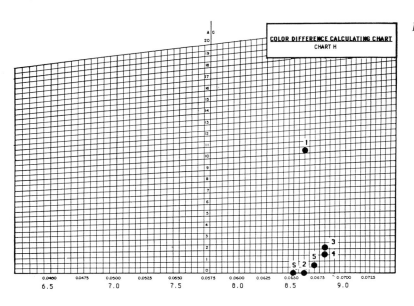

Figure 4. Red reference tile.

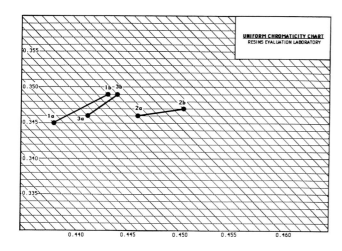

Figure 5. Area D-1A, reds.

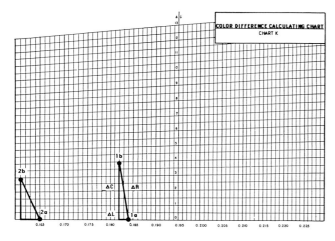

Figure 6. Area D-1A, locations 1 and 2.

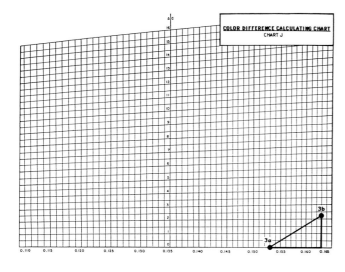

Figure 7. Area D-1A, location 3.

First Report on Analyses of Samples

Frank Preusser

Salt and plaster samples from the wall paintings in the tomb of Nefertari were analyzed at the Getty Conservation Institute by Abel Rodarte, Research Assistant; Donald R. Dietrich, Associate Scientist; Jack Gromek, Research Fellow; and Michael Schilling, Assistant Scientist. The advice and assistance of Prof. Feisal A. Esmael of the Egyptian Antiquities Organization, of Prof. Saleh Ahmed Saleh of Cairo University, and Dr. John Twilley of the Los Angeles County Museum of Art contributed significantly to the preparation of this report.

This report presents the first results of sample analyses, which are still in progress. Four sets of samples were examined: (1) salt samples selected on the basis of crystallization appearance taken from different locations in the tomb. These were selected by Prof. Esmael, Mr. Schilling, and the author; (2) plaster and paint samples from a box in a niche in inner room Q (see plan of the tomb), selected by Prof. Esmael, Mr. Schilling, and the author; (3) salt, plaster, and paint samples selected by Prof. Saleh and brought to the Getty Conservation Institute in November 1986; and (4) "gypsum" obtained from a mineral vein in a tomb east of the tomb of Nefertari.

Purpose of the Analyses

The analyses were undertaken to verify previous findings (Jaksch, Saleh et al.) and provide additional information on the composition and deterioration of the plasters and paint layers in the tomb, thereby establishing a basis for the planning of future painting treatment.

In addition to the chemical, crystallographic, and microscopic analyses, color measurements were made in the tomb in September 1986. These measurements will serve as a reference point in a monitoring program during the next years.

Procedure

All samples were first examined microscopically, using a Wild M8 stereomicroscope with a magnification of 5-60x and a Leitz Orthoplan with a maximum magnification of 700x. As necessary, microchemical analyses will be performed.

X-ray diffraction analyses were conducted using a Siemens D500 X-ray diffractometer. It was originally anticipated that the analysis would be performed with a Bragg-Brentano goniometer, using a position-sensitive detector (PSD). Difficulties with the multichannel analyzer required that a Gandolfi and Debye-Scherrer camera be used. The diffractograms were recorded on film, and the film was measured with a densitometer connected to a DEC PDP 11/23 computer (this procedure resulted in a slightly higher error in the peak positions). The diffractograms were then searched by computer against the JCPDS files using the Hanawalt method. In addition to the computer searches, reference diffractograms prepared by the Getty Conservation Institute were used to interpret the diffractograms. Future work will include the use of the goniometer and PSD.

A JEOL 733 Superprobe (maximum magnification of 100,000x, resolution 70Å), equipped with a Tracor Northern energy dispersive X-ray spectrometer, three wavelength dispersive spectrometers, and an image-processing program were used for imaging and microanalysis.

Results

The salt crystallization in the tomb has various appearances: thick layers (up to 15mm) of dense salt crystallization in rock cleavages and under plaster; "curly" thick crystals in rock cleavages, under plaster, and on the surface of paint layers;" hairlike"crystals on the surface of paint layers; and "cubic" crystals on the surface of paint layers.

The salt samples have been analyzed by X-ray diffraction. All salt samples (independent of their appearance) consist of sodium chloride (NaCl), of relative high purity. Figures 1, 2 are examples of the diffraction patterns. Although the grounded samples were rotated in the camera, their preferred orientation can still be observed. Figure 3 is an overlay of the diffraction patterns of salt samples of the types 2, 3.

One sample of type 1 (thick, dense layers) taken by Prof. Saleh (sample NEF7) has been studied with the electron-beam microprobe. The results are given in Appendix 1. To collect more data about this sample and study the question of whether one can distinguish discrete events of crystal growth (which may be attributed to individual rain events), thin sections of the samples will be prepared.

Only a few plaster samples have been studied to date. X-ray diffraction analysis shows the presence of three different types of plasters (also previously reported): lime, gypsum, and clay. All plasters, however, contain additional components, and the term *"gypsum"* is used for anhydrous and hydrated forms of $CaSO_4$. Detailed information will be given in a future report after more samples have been analyzed.

Sample NEF8 (plaster from the ceiling of sarcophagus chamber K taken by Prof. Saleh) was studied comprehensively with the electron-beam microprobe. The results are given in Appendix 2. While it was assumed that the weakness of the plaster is caused by salt crystallizing in the pores of the plaster, no salt was detected in the plaster. Further analyses are being discussed with Prof. Saleh.

The pigments in the Egyptian tombs of the Pharaonic period have been extensively studied, most recently by a German group (Jaksch et al.). It was therefore considered unnecessary to repeat this work. Some pigments, however, were identified during the salt and plaster analyses.

A salt sample from a niche in east side room O contained white particles identified as huntite ($Mg_3Ca[CO_3]_4$). Their morphology suggests that huntite has not been added as white pigment but has been formed on the paint surface (similar to the crystallization of sodium chloride). This possibility will be further analyzed.

The pigments in a blue sample were identified as cuprorivaite (Egyptian blue, ($CaCuSi_4O_{10}$) and calcite ($CaCO_3$). One blue sample, which appeared black, was examined microscopically. The change of appearance was attributed to an organic coating. The composition of this coating is to be determined.

The mineral vein in an adjacent tomb has been identified as anhydrite ($CaSO_4$). Figure 4 is an overlay of this sample and the reference diffractogram.

Future Analysis

Planned future work will include: (1) continued characterization of the different plasters by X-ray diffraction and electron-beam microanalysis; (2) preparation of thin sections of paint and plaster samples and characterization by electron-beam microanalysis; (3) study of thin sections of salt type 1; (4) analysis of potentially present organic binding media, using microchemical methods and FTIR. Other methods will be applied if necessary; (5) evaluation of the potential value of other types of analysis (e.g., stable-isotope analysis); and (6) material analysis to answer specific questions related to the conservation of the wall paintings.

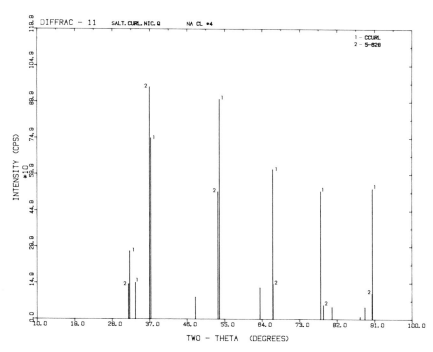

Figure 1. Comparison of salt hair (1) with JCPDS NaCl standard (2).

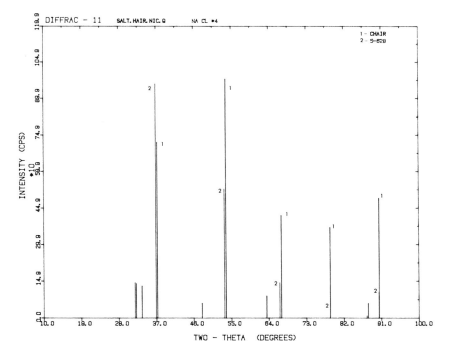

Figure 2. Comparison of salt curl (1) with JCPDS NaCl standard (2).

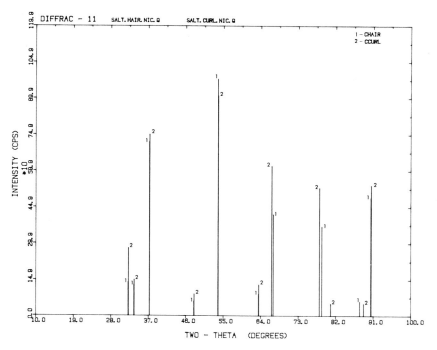

Figure 3. Comparison of salt hair (1) with salt curl (2).

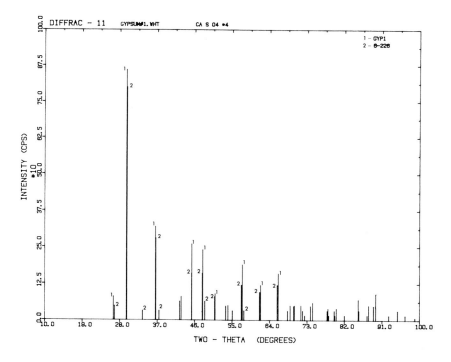

Figure 4. Comparison of gypsum vein (1) with JCPDS gypsum standard (2).

Appendix 1: Sample NEF7 from the Tomb of Nefertari

Sample NEF7 is the halite bundle selected by Prof. Saleh for examination for nucleation sites. Since the exact orientation of the sample, wall rock, and painted surface to each other is not known, a theory on grain development and growth must include some speculation about what side was in contact with the wall. The halite grains are elongated perpendicular to the wall. The orientation of the photographs is such that the wall and paint surface are vertical.

No iron or titanium zoning was found in a line scan across the sample. Preliminary textural analysis suggests that the halite formed at the limestone-halite interface and grew outward. Thus the limestone was presumably the rock wall and the source of the saline solution. Further optical examination after preparation of a thin section will verify the textural relationship.

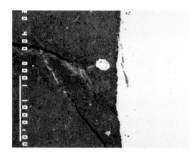

Figure 5. Backscattered electron image of sample NEF 7 showing the limestone-halite interface. Note the fractures and circular feature in the limestone on the left. The boundaries of the halite grains are barely visible on the right. Which edge was toward the wall is unknown but the sample is oriented so that the edges are vertical. (Scale bar is 1 mm.)

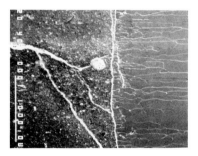

Figure 6. Secondary plus backscattered electron image of same view as figure 5. Compositional contrast is greatly reduced but the topography is enhanced. The halite grains are elongated perpendicular to the rock wall. Since the direction normal to the wall would have least stress, growth most likely occurred from the wall outward. (Scale bar is 1 mm.)

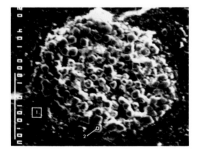

Figure 7. Secondary plus backscattered electron image of the circular feature in figure 5. Spectrum 1 shows the presence in the surrounding matrix of calcium, silicon, chlorine, aluminum, sodium, potassium, magnesium, and iron. Thus the matrix probably contains Ca-(±Mg)-carbonate, at least one aluminosilicate, and perhaps somes halite. Spectrum 2 indicates that the moderately well-formed crystals in the circular feature contain mostly iron, probably in the form of iron oxide. The other elements may be from the surrounding matrtix and not from the crystals. Their rhombohedral morphology and composition suggest that the crystals are hematite. (Scale bar is 0.1 mm.)

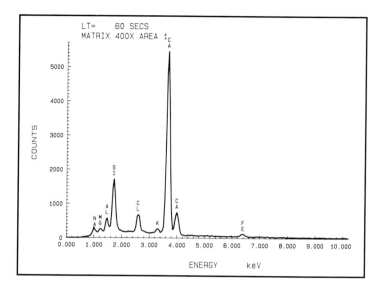

Spectrum 1. EDS analysis of matrix shown as area 1 in figure 7.

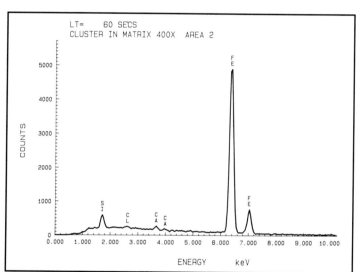

Spectrum 2. EDS analysis of grain marked area 2 in figure 7.

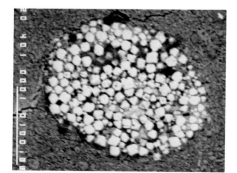

Figure 8. Backscattered electron image showing compositional contrast for the same area as figure 7. The fine-grained character of the matrix is visible and suggests an abundance of clay in the limestone. The compact, friable nature of the matrix when examined by hand also indicates the presence of clay. Scale bar is 0.1 mm.)

Figure 9. Backscattered electron image of halite near the interface with the limestone matrix. A small piece of the limestone extends into the view from the left, near the scale bar. The grains tend to form sets of relatively equal lengths with lines separating the sets being roughly parallel to the interface. The grains are shortest at the interface. (Scale bar is 1 mm.)

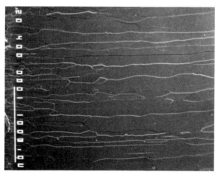

Figure 10. Secondary plus backscattered electron image of the same view as figure 9. Most of the black spots in figure 9 are actually pores, as is more easily seen here. (Scale bar is 1 mm.)

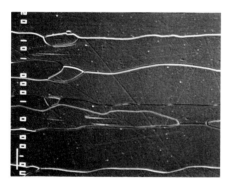

Figure 11. Secondary plus backscattered electron image of the central region in figure 9 showing detail of the halite grain boundaries. (Scale bar is 0.1 mm.)

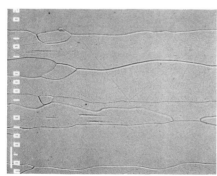

Figure 12. Backscattered electron image of same view in figure 11. Apparently no other phase is present even along the grain boundaries. The halite is essentially free of inclusions. (Scale bar is 0.1 mm.)

Appendix 2: Sample NEF8 from the Tomb of Nefertari

Sample NEF8 was brought by Prof. Saleh to the Getty Conservation Institute for examination of the pores for halite crystals. The sample is a chip from the ceiling of sarcophagus chamber K, from a rapidly deteriorating section. Prof. Saleh believes that halite crystallization in the plaster pores may be contributing to the deterioration. The attached images from a freshly broken surface show that neither halite nor other deposits are present in the pores. If halite is present it must be intermingled with the plaster because the linings of the pores have the same appearance as the freshly broken surface of the plaster. Spectrum 1 is an Energy Dispersive Spectroscopy analysis of the small area between the pores marked in figure 7. The plaster contains calcium, silicon, magnesium, aluminum, iron, and potassium. Several phases are present. They are most likely carbonates, aluminosilicates, and possibly some iron oxides.

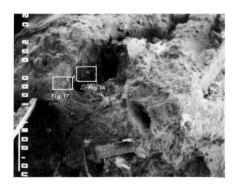

Figure 13. Secondary plus backscattered electron image of sample NEF8. Pores of various sizes are visible. The largest one will be investigated in figures 13-21. Four pieces of plant fibers (straw?) extend from the plaster. The piece just below center was bent when the sample was broken to expose the fresh surface. The plant fibers are oriented with their flat sides parallel. (Scale bar is 1 mm.)

Figure 14. Secondary plus backscattered electron image of left side of the large pore in figure 13. The very bright areas show the effects of charging in regions where the conductive gold coating is incomplete. Figure 15 shows a closer view of the lower left two-thirds of this view. (Scale bar is 0.1 mm.)

Figure 15. Secondary plus backscattered electron image showing closer view of the area in figure 14. The grains are nearly spherical, and no cubic halite crystals are visible. (Scale bar is 0.1 mm.)

Figure 16. Secondary plus backscattered electron image showing close-up of grains in the center of figure 15. No cubic halite crystals are visible. A small rhombohedral crystal just above center is barely discernible, but it is most likely a carbonate (calcite?). (Scale bar is 0.01 mm.)

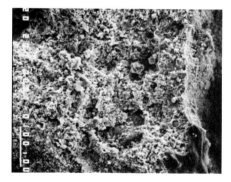

Figure 17. Secondary plus backscattered electron image of the fresh surface indicated in figure 13. The edge of the pore can be seen running down the right third of the view. The texture of the surface is similar to the wall of the pore. (Scale bar is 0.1 mm.)

Figure 18. Secondary plus backscattered electron image showing close-up of central field of figure 17. The rhombohedral crystals seem to be more abundant, but no cubic halite crystals are present. (Scale bar is 0.01 mm.)

Figure 19. Secondary plus backscattered electron image showing a slightly different view from figure 13. Two smaller pores near the upper-right corner will be shown in the following two figures. (Scale bar is 1 mm.)

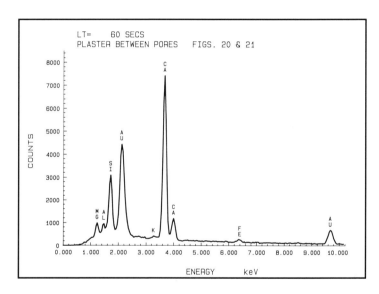

Spectrum 3. EDS analysis of freshly broken plaster between the pores indicated in figure 19.

Figure 20. Secondary plus backscattered electron image of the pore indicated in figure 19. A spider web-like feature and piece of plant fiber (straw?) can be seen, but no halite cubes are present. (Scale bar is 0.01 mm.)

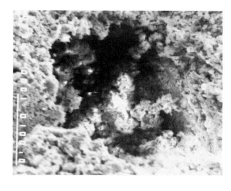

Figure 21. Secondary plus backscattered electron image of the second pore marked in figure 19. The very bright areas indicate charging. No halite cubes are present in this pore. (Scale bar is 0.1 mm.)

References

Berry, Leonard G. et al., eds. 1982. *Powder Diffraction File: Joint Committee on Powder Diffraction Standards.* Philadelphia.

Deer, W. A., R.A. Howie, and J. Zussman. 1976. *An Introduction to the Rock Forming Minerals.* London.

Delbourgo, S. 1976. "Application of the Electron Microprobe to the Study of Some Italian Paintings of the Fourteenth to the Sixteenth Century." *Conservation and Restoration of Pictorial Art*, N. Brommelle and P. Smith, eds. London.

El-Goresy, A. et al. 1986. "Ancient Pigments in Wall Paintings of Egyptian Tombs and Temples, an Archaeometric Project." Heidelberg.

Goldstein, J.I. et al. 1981. *Scanning Electron Microscopy and X-ray Microanalysis.* New York and London.

Michalowski, A. (ed). 1973. "The Tomb of Nefertari: Problems of Conserving Wall Paintings, Diagnosing the State of Preservation and Conservator'sProposals." Conservation Information Center, Working Group of the State Ateliers for the Preservation of Historical Property. Warsaw.

Pigments, Plaster and Salts Analyses

Saleh Ahmed Saleh

This is a revised report of part of the work carried out by the author, given in an unpublished book-form report in 1980 under the title "The Tomb of Nefertari: Deterioration, phenomena, factors and treatment techniques."

The present work is one of the earliest comprehensive X-ray analyses of the materials used in the wall paintings of the tomb of Nefertari and was planned to provide information needed for the final conservation project. X-ray diffraction and X-ray fluorescence were used, as well as classical wet chemical analysis and normal microscopic investigation.

The X-ray diffraction scans were taken by a Philips X-ray diffractometer under the following operating conditions: Ge.38kV, 16 mA, copper radiation and Ni-filter, Gon. Sc.v. 2°/min., chart v. 10 mm/min , counting rate 4×10^2 or 1×10^3 c.p.s., using a proportional counter. A Philips X-ray spectrometer was used when only a tungsten tube was available. A LiF analyzing crystal or EDDT crystal with vacuum were used with a scintillation counter. Other operating conditions were similar to those of the diffractometry. Classical wet chemical analysis was applied on numerous plaster and salt samples but was not used for the examination of the pigment materials. Two types of microscopes were used: the stereo Wild binocular microscope and the Zeiss polarized microscope with automatic photographic attachment.

In this report only a few, selected X-ray scans are published for illustration purposes. All the scans can be obtained from the Egyptian Antiquities Organization or the Getty Conservation Institute. Pigment materials were examined in conditions identical to those on the tomb walls; 2x1 cm rectangular fragments with suitable thickness were mounted in the X-ray diffractometer or spectrometer specimen holders.

Blue pigment. The microscopic examination indicated blue transparent irregular grains mixed with other minerals. The XRD analysis indicated a rather impure form of cuprorivaite, known as Egyptian Blue ($CaCuSi_4O_{10}$), mixed with wollastonite, α-quartz, tridymite calcite and other impurities.

The Egyptian Blue or blue frit is a synthetic pigment introduced into wall paintings in Egypt during the Fourth Dynasty and used until the late Roman period. It solved the problem of deficiency of azurite ($2CuCO_3 \bullet Cu(OH)_2$) as a natural alternative for the blue pigment. The chemical composition, crystal structure and methods of manufacturing the pigment have attracted the attention of numerous authors. The XRF scan taken with the LiF crystal showed the presence of copper as the main colorant metal, and traces of iron, strontium and tin.

Bluish green pigment. This pigment appeared under the microscope in the form of irregular transparent bluish green grains mixed with several other minerals. The XRD scan showed the presence of a good amount of α-quartz, calcite, anhydrite, and wollastonite, together with the pigment material. The XRF scan taken with the LiF crystal showed the same colorant metals as in the blue pigment, together with a trace amount of arsenic. The author was successful in producing a blue pigment with variable shades, but was unable to prepare a green pigment with a crystal structure identical to the ancient one.

The artificial green pigment was quite rare, possibly because of the ease and abundance of natural green malachite ($CuCO_3 \bullet Cu(OH)_2$).

Red pigment. The analysis mentioned in the Polish report indicated the presence of Fe^{3+} and concluded that the material is ferric oxide. The XRD scan showed the pigment material to be hematite (α-Fe_2O_3), but was difficult to read because the signal was almost totally masked by sodium chloride where the reflection of α - because hematite has a very low intensity. The pattern shows the presence of gypsum ($CaSO_4 \bullet 2H_2O$) for the first time in all investigated samples. The XRF scan with LiF crystal clearly showed the presence of a high amount of iron.

Yellow pigment. The samples showed the presence of two different materials used for the yellow pigment. The first one is hydrated iron oxide, known as limonite, while the other is the arsenic sulphide mineral known as orpiment (As_2S_3). Unfortunately the diffraction lines of the orpiment were greatly masked by the presence of superficial sodium chloride crystals seen in the XRD scan. The high amount of arsenic in the sample, however, is clearly seen in the XRF scan. Iron is present because the specimen is a yellow ground with reddish brown strips.

White pigment. Samples examined for this pigment were of white ground free from any other colored scenes. The surface is covered with a film of sodium chloride crystals, which greatly affected the intensity of other material reflections. The XRD scan shows sodium chloride, calcite, and anhydrite, as well as minute traces of huntite ($CaCO_3 \bullet 3MgCO_3$), which is not an uncommon trace in white grounds of lime origin. The XRF analysis did not indicate any noteworthy elements other than minute traces of iron and strontium, which are persistent elements in all lime plasters.

The wall paintings in this tomb are a good example of the tempera technique. The physical characteristics (looseness of pigment grains, washability and effect of aqueous solution) supposes the use of arabic gum or animal glue solutions as media for applying the coloring materials. This was also assumed by the Polish and UNESCO reports; the subject may need more detailed scientific analysis for a final conclusion. It is very important for future restoration work to consider that the tempera paintings are of the plaster high relief technique, which is very uncommon in Egyptian wall paintings.

Plaster Samples

The tomb and the surrounding limestone mother rock were subject to tectonic movements that resulted in complete rock fracturing along three inclined planes of almost rhombohedral form; one of these planes is more obvious and dominant.

To overcome the difficulty in preparing the cut wall surface for painting, the artist had to use a combination of clay, gypsum and lime plasters of various thicknesses depending on the treated depths of wall surfaces. This can be clearly noticed from close observation of the wall paintings and from visual inspection of the accumulated plaster fragments stored in the side room of the burial chamber.

Sample I. This was taken from the detached plaster in the ceiling of the burial chamber.

1. Inner ground layer. The sample appeared to be of whitish yellow and almost loose, coarse sand grains. The looseness and weakness of the layer was assumed by the author to be the result of intergranular growth of sodium chloride crystals. The XRD scan, however, clearly showed the absence of any salts. This fact was confirmed later by Donald Dietrich at the Getty Conservation Institute, using the electron-beam microprobe. The sample is composed of α-quartz sand grains constituting the material body, while the binders are calcium carbonate and a very small amount of anhydrous calcium sulphate (anhydrite). These results were confirmed by wet chemical analysis.

2. The materials appeared to have fewer but finer sand grains and were more whitish. The XRD scan indicates the presence of a higher amount of calcium carbonate than calcium sulphate anhydrous (anhydrite) and an unidentified component besides α-quartz.

Sample II. The sample was a very small fragment that had fallen in 1986 from the left wall in the burial chamber over the mastaba. This sample is important because it provides information about the nature of gypsum plaster in the walls where the plaster is highly cracked and dangerously detached from the rock wall. The specimen consists of an inner clay with chopped straw layer and an outer white fine gypsum layer.

1. Outer white layer. The XRD scan (figure 13) clearly indicates that the sample is essentially composed of anhydrous calcium sulphate or (anhydrite) with sand grains, α-quartz and much smaller amount of calcium carbonate. Surprisingly, there are no traces of sodium chloride crystals. The results confirmed the author's assumption that proper gypsum plaster of hydrated calcium sulphate ($CaSO_4$ $2H_2O$) was used and has completely transformed into anhydrite. This transformation caused a large decrease in plaster volume, more apparently in the plane parallel to the wall surface, which led to random cracking and detachment of plaster from the walls.

2. Inner ground layer. The XRD analysis revealed calcareous clay with a significant amount of sand grains. Visual inspection clearly revealed that chopped straw had been added to the clay.

3. Outer painted surface. The surface of the plaster contained homogeneous bright yellow paint, which was examined without grinding. A film of sodium chloride salt was detected, as it was in all other pigments (see XRD scans of examined pigments), and a very small amount of anhydrite and α-quartz was also detected.

Sample III. This sample was taken from the outer upper edge of the mastaba on the left side of the upper chamber. As expected, it consisted of inner coarse and outer fine ground layers.

1. Inner ground layer. The XRD analysis showed that the sample contained a significant amount of coarse sand grains, calcium carbonate, and traces of anhydrite. Its XRF scan showed the presence of calcium and traces of iron with minute traces of titanium, potassium, manganese, and copper.

2. Outer ground layer. This appeared to consist of more fine grains that were whitish in color. XRD analysis shows the presence primarily of anhydrite with lesser amounts of quartz sand and calcite. The XRF scan taken with EDDT crystal, under vacuum, did not reveal great differences from that of the inner ground layer. The wet chemical analysis confirmed the presence of carbonate in the binder of the inner layer and the sulphate in the outer one.

Salt Crystallizations

Because of the very dry environment inside the tomb, evaporation and crystallization phenomena are expected to take place at the solid-gas surfaces. These can be on the outer surfaces of the painted plaster, behind the detached thick plaster layer, or in fissure cavities and fracture planes in the limestone wall surfaces. The latter case created huge masses of well crystallized salt; a respresentative sample was examined using the electron-beam microprobe at the Getty Conservation Institute. The lateral growth of the curled and hairlike crystals formed on the painted plaster surfaces have completely destroyed the colored scenes, leaving the inner ground layer exposed. This is generally the case on the lateral right and left walls of the upper chamber.

Crystallization of salt on rock walls behind thick plaster layers have led to the formation of very strong crystal bundles that have detached large areas of paintings and plaster layers in the burial chamber. Formation of numerous salt pustules have destroyed the beautiful condition of wall paintings in the side rooms of the burial chamber, and represent another form of salt problem.

Another particularly significant result of salt crystallization is the very fine film or unseen salt pits on surfaces of the wall paintings in areas which otherwise appear to be in good condition. This phenomenon was discovered only when the author tried to examine pigment materials using XRD of untouched specimen surfaces (see XRD scans of pigments).

The intensity of the (200) sodium chloride reflection seemed to have the greater part of the total intensity and this convinced the author to assume that the fine salt crystals are oriented with their cube faces parallel to the specimen surface.

During his visit to the laboratories of the Getty Conservation Institute, the author attempted, along with Donald Dietrich and Abel Rodarte, to use the normal microscope and electron-beam microprobe to follow the square shape of crystal cube faces in one sample, but was unable to achieve any positive results. During the visit, the author left six pigment samples and one plaster ground layer from the ceiling of the burial chamber to be examined with the electron-beam microprobe.

The presence of such types of salt crystals should nevertheless be considered during preparation for the final conservation treatment of the wall paintings.

Examination of numerous salt samples by wet chemical, XRD, and XRF analyses revealed that whenever the samples are far from stone or plaster contaminants, they are composed of pure sodium chloride.

Summary

For future cleaning, consolidation, and restoration of the wall paintings, the following points should be considered: (1) variation in materials and thicknesses of inner and outer ground plaster layers; (2) looseness and washability of pigments in general, and specifically the coarse-grained synthetic materials; (3) the presence of sodium chloride film or pits on the wall paintings in areas which seem to be in good condition; (4) variation in form, shape, strength, and locations of sodium chloride crystals; and (5) complete transformation of gypsum anhydrite in areas where the dominance of gypsum plaster has created a cracking, detachment, and loss of cohesion.

Figure 1. Effect of surface crystallization between inner and outer plaster layers.

Figure 2. Effect of lateral growth of surface crystal.

Figure 3. Crystal bundles from limestone walls pushing away plaster and paints.

Figure 4. Random cracking and detaching of plaster layer because of transformation of gypsum into anhydrite.

Figure 5. Crystal bundle growing from limestone pores pushing away plaster layer, burial chamber.

Figure 6. Typical crystal bundle in stone fracture cavity, side room, burial chamber.

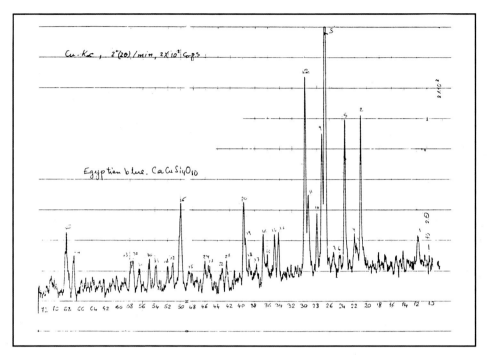

Figure 7. X-ray diffraction scan of blue pigment, burial chamber ceiling.

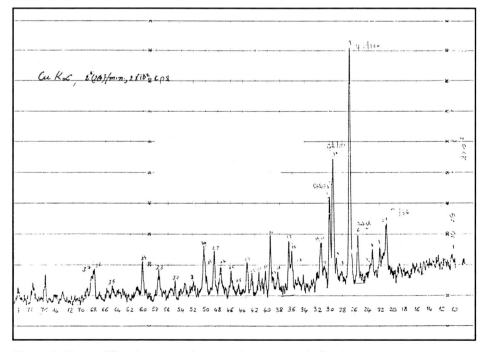

Figure 8. X-ray diffraction scan of green pigment, burial chamber.

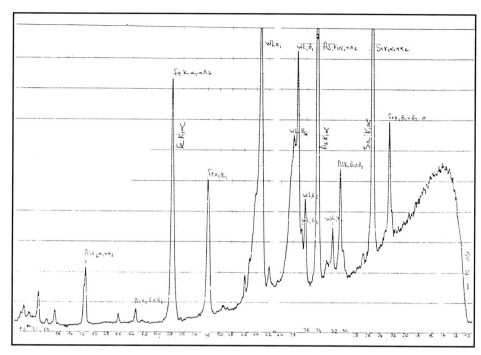

Figure 9. X-ray diffraction scan of yellow with red stripes, burial chamber.

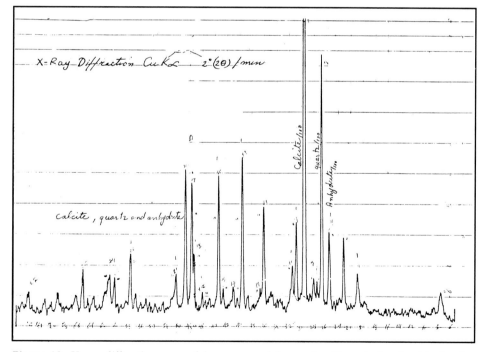

Figure 10. X-ray diffraction scan of inner ground layer of ceiling plaster, burial chamber.

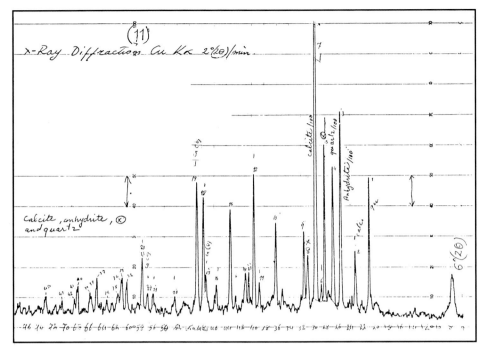

Figure 11. X-ray diffraction scan of outer ground layer of ceiling plaster, burial chamber.

References

Burns, G. and K. M. Wilson-Yang. 1981. "The Tomb of Nefertari, Valley of the Queens and its Conservation Problems." Preliminary report, Archaeometric Laboratory, Toronto.

Lucas, A. 1962. *Ancient Egyptian Materials and Industries*. Fourth edition. London.

Michalowski, A. ed. 1973. "The Tomb of Queen Nefertari: Problems of Conserving Wall Paintings." *PKZ*. Warsaw.

Mora, P., L. Mora, and P. Phillipot. 1984. *Conservation of Wall Paintings*. London.

Nicolini, L. and P. Santini. 1958. *Bolletino del Istituto Centrale di Restauro*. Rome.

Pabst, A. 1959. "Structure of Some Tetragonal Sheet Silicates." *Acta Cryst.* 12, p. 733.

Plenderleith, H. J., P. Mora, G. Torraca, and G. de Guichen. 1970. "The Tomb of Nefertari, United Arab Republic - Conservation Problems." UNESCO Report, Section II, Serial No.1914/BMS. RD/CLT. Paris.

Saleh, S. A. 1980. "The Tomb of Nefertari, Deterioration Phenomena, Factors and Treatment Techniques." In Arabic. Cairo University, Giza.

Saleh, S. A. 1981-87. "Treatment and Restoration of Mural Paintings." Year-long course for third-year students, Department of Conservation, Cairo University, Giza.

Saleh, S. A., Z. Iskander, A. El Masry, and F. M. Helmi. 1974. "Some Ancient Egyptian Pigments." *Recent Advances in Science and Technology of Materials*, Vol. 3. New York and London.

Nondestructive Testing

Modesto Montoto

This study focuses on the location of voids under apparently sound paint layers and is intended to diagnose the state of adhesion or decohesion between the rock and plaster that supports the paintings in the tomb of Nefertari. The detachment of the plaster from the rock stems from the mechanical stresses developed along their interface during the crystallization of large salt crystals. This crystallization leaves empty spaces along the rock-plaster interface. Investigations of the tomb must be performed by means of nondestructive tests. No other group attempting to solve a similar problem has yet been located.

Several prerequisite conditions must be considered in this study:

1. Vibrations and stresses on the paintings are prohibited.

2. The nondestructive character of any test or instrument to be applied on the tomb must be verified in another tomb.

3. Detailed information on the stratigraphy, lithology, geochemistry, and joint pattern of the site must be provided. Many open joints are in the tomb, and the width between the rock and detached plaster may be larger than anticipated.

4. The plaster nature, its properties and thickness, are unknown. A very rough surface delimits the contact between the plaster and rock. Plaster and rock seem to share similar physical properties. These physical similarities are very important in nondestructive testing, for instance, in the acoustic impedance monitored in ultrasonic methods.

5. Nondestructive testing methods must be carefully selected. Most methods (density and neutron logs) are very valuable, for instance, in the evaluation of rock density and porosity. Unfortunately the restrictions imposed by the nature of the tomb prohibit their present application in these investigations.

Among the various theoretically applicable nondestructive methods only a few can be considered. To make certain that the selected methods are correct and guarantee reasonable results when applied in the tomb of Nefertari, they must be examined under consistent laboratory experimentation.

Nondestructive testing methods are primarily based on monitoring a given signal and detection of significant variations. Three general methods can be considered here to detect incompletely refilled spaces along the rock-plaster interface (the void spaces are expected to represent a discontinuity in the behavior of the signal). Methods based on any particular phenomenon (radioactivity or thermal irradiation, for instance), which conditions a spontaneous and continuous signal from the rock, are not appropriate in the testing of calcareous stones found in the tomb. Methods based on monitoring any artificial signal injected into the wall, after traveling through the plaster and rock underneath, are not applicable. The signals passing through open spaces will be highly attenuated compared with those traveling through solid material. In these transparent methods the signal introduced could be an electric current, ultrasound waves, or X-ray. Obviously all are impractical in this tomb, excavated in the mountain, because there is no way to receive the injected signals after their passage through the plaster and outer layer of rock.

The author had intended originally to drill on the wall on which would be placed a transducer, which would emit ultrasounds to be monitored on the paintings in the vicinity of the emitter. This would represent a complete mapping of the wall to detect areas opaque to the traveling waves.

The most appropriate methods for this task are based on the monitoring of signals injected into the plaster and reflected on the discontinuities found in their way. Because of the physical constraints of the tomb and time limitations, the echo method of monitoring reflected ultrasounds was selected as the most appropriate nondestructive testing method.

The ultrasound frequencies to be used in this method are especially significant. Other technical aspects such as coupling, attenuation, echo scattering, and acoustic impedance must be carefully considered.

Low frequencies lack definition and imply a lower attenuation, but they can jump over the narrow open spaces (detached zones), avoiding a good echo. High frequencies allow a very good definition and best echo conditions; they are more directional but show higher attenuation. An experimental study with different transducers is necessary to investigate the most appropriate frequency (that is, an acceptable attenuation and high reflectance in the detached areas). To reproduce the dry coupling conditions between the transducer and wall paintings, a tool must be designed and constructed.

Water, oil, and epoxy are generally used as couplants to obtain a good transmission of ultrasounds from the transducer into the material and vice versa. To avoid damaging the sound paintings a dry coupling must be used; unfortunately the emitted signal then becomes highly attenuated into the material. The damping of the emitted waves in amplitude and frequency is very high in these extremely porous materials (2-10 cm is the expected average length traveled by the waves).

A very rough surface delimits the contact between the plaster and rock in the tomb. The ultrasounds emitted from the wall paintings do not arrive perpendicularly to the detached surfaces, causing an echo to spread widely in many directions, thereby making its location ambiguous.

Some physical properties of the plaster and rock seem to be very similar. The acoustic impedance of both materials has been evaluated theoretically in the range of 7-10 kg/m^2. This is a favorable situation, because a high-impedance contrast exists between the detached and adhered zones. In the adhered zones the waves travel through the plaster-rock interface and reflected waves are not expected to be formed; from the detached areas only reflected waves are expected.

To study the plaster-rock detachment experimentally, specimens were prepared and tested using various nondestructive ultrasonic testing methods. The plaster had been assumed to be homogeneous, that is, having no variations in density and composition along directions parallel and perpendicular to the walls.

Several experts in the field were consulted. Carlos Valdecantos, Construcciones Aeronáuticas S.A., Madrid, Spain, offered advice regarding the ultrasonic analysis of the mechanical impedance between the detached and nondetached areas of the specimens. The phase and amplitude analysis does not discriminate among the detached areas. Frequencies of up to 9 KHz were used.

José Miguel Alvarez, Instituto Nacional de Técnica Aeroespacial, Madrid, Spain, offered advice regarding ultrasonic tests on transmission and echo (pitch-catch and single-transducer method with frequencies of about 500 KHz.

Dr. Juan Antonio Gallego Suárez, Instituto de Acústica, Consejo Superior de Investigaciones Cientificas, Madrid, Spain, served as advisor on transducers.

Prof. Robert D. Adams, Department of Mechanical Engineering, University of Bristol, United Kingdom, developed a Tapometer prototype instrument to implement the coin-tap technique (presented at the Eleventh World Conference on Nondestructive Testing, 1985). This technique is based on the different sounds produced when whole and defective areas of a structure are tapped. The instrument provides quantitative and recordable results and has been used to detect delaminations among other material structural defects. Because of the variable thickness of the plaster (up to several centimeters), Prof. Adams suggested that a relatively high impact will be necessary to excite the detached areas. He suggested the use of a Schmidt hammer (a sclerometer to measure hardness in rocks). Such impacting, however, will damage the wall paintings, and the technique must be considered as unacceptable.

Also offering advice were Dott.ssa Marisa Tabasso,Director, Laboratorio di Proba di Materiale, Istituto Centrale di Restauro, Rome, Italy;and Guido Chiesura, CND, Rome, Italy.

James D. Leaird, Acoustic Emission Technology Co., Sacramento, California, USA, has modified an acousto-ultrasonic technique developed by the National Aeronautics and Space Administration to nondestructively inspect materials. The modified equipment has been applied to masonry structures. Flaws were located and their severity ranked (*Journal of Acoustic Emission* 4 [1985]). A Schmidt hammer was used to generate the pulsed impact signal (measurements along large areas of masonry structures were carried out in this study). This lightweight, portable instrument, operating with a dry coupling probe, 40 KHz to 1.5 MHz band width, pulse mode, in steps, from 1 to 2,000 pulses per second and duration from 8 to 180 seconds may be applicable to the treatment of the tomb paintings. To verify its applicability a specimen was sent to Mr. Leaird in Sacramento. The attenuation of the ultrasounds, generated by the nondestructive pulse mode when traveling through the plaster, must be analyzed.

References

Case Studies in the Conservation of Stone and Wall Paintings.

Preprints of the Contributions to the Bologna Congress, 21-26 September 1986. Ten papers in which the phenomenon of plaster-rock adhesion was examined. In all the plaster and/or pictorial layer was detached.

Agrawal, O. P. "Conservation problems of Ajanta wall paintings." Pp. 86-88.

Arnold, A.; A. Küng and K. Zehnder. "Deterioration and preservation of Carolingian and medieval mural paintings in the Müstair Convent (Switzerland). Part 1: Decay, mechanisms, and preservation." Pp. 190-94.

Bandini, F. et al. "The restoration of Domenico Ghirlandaio's frescoes in the Cappella Maggiore of S. Maria Novella in Florence: Problems, practical work, results." Pp. 186-89.

Eastham, M. R. "Conservation of the Carewe-Pole Monument." Pp. 170-73.

Horky, J. "Restoration of wall paintings in a small chapel near Fribourg." Pp. 44-47.

Mora, L. et al. "A coordinated methodology for the treatment and study of the peristile garden wall of the House of Menander, Pompeii: An interim report." Pp. 38-43. The decohesion below the surface was apparently identified in this case by "visual inspection, manipulation of the surface, and by tapping." The problem seems to be irrelevant for the authors as no comments on the method and results are included in the paper.

Nishiura, T. "Conservation of rock-cliff sculptures in Japan." Pp. 155-58.

Park, D. and D. Perry. "Rochester Cathedral: Conservation of the crypt vault paintings." Pp. 182-85.

Schwartzbaum, P. M., W. Na Songkla, and I. Massari. "The conservation of mural paintings in Thailand." Pp. 90- 95.

Stefenaggi, M., J. Vouve, and I. Dangas. "Climatic, hydrogeological and scientific study of the wall paintings of the crypt of Saint Savin sur Gartempe (Vienne, France)." Pp. 96-100.

First International Conference on Nondestructive Testing in Conservation of Works of Art. Rome, 27-29 October 1983.

Bonarrigo, A. C. Calcagno, and V. Fassina. "Il degrada dei mosaici della Basilica di Maria Assunta di Torcello: Risultati preliminari di un metodo non distruttivo per valutare l'eterogeneitá dello intonaco sottostante i mosaici." Pp. III/3.1. In this study the detached areas of a mosaic were located by listening to the variation in the tone of a low- frequency signal applied on the surface. The coin-tap test is also impractical in the tomb of Nefertari.

Canella, G. "Controllo non distruttivo e moduli elastici di componenti lapidei. La Fontana Maggiore di Perugia." Pp. I/7.1-17. This paper describes the use of transmission-ultrasonic tests to verify rock and the concrete adhesion. Transmission methods are excluded in the Nefertari project.

Esposti, W., S. Levrero, and G. Stella. "Analisi delle irregolaritá di strati superficiali di murature portanti opere d'arte tramite termografia infrarossa e auscultazione dinamica." Pp. I/11.1-14. A very interesting problem, similar to that of the tomb of Nefertari, has appeared in the works of restoration of the church of Sant'Angelo in Milan. The state of adhesion between the antique plaster and the masonry wall showed significant differences as observed by percussion. This paper deals with the problem of locating "anomalous situations both in the masonry and, above all, in the plaster and its state of adhesion to the wall surface," using infrared vision and ultrasonic auscultation. According to the authors both techniques provided good results in the detection of detached plaster.

The infrared technique was also applied to the wall painting *The Last Supper* by Leonardo da Vinci as reported in this paper. The walls were heated by a small infrared lamp located about 1 m from the wall surface for about thirty to sixty seconds.

Although no data about the temperature reached by the outer-wall surface during the heating are reported, the authors claim, after Cesini et al., 1979, ("Rivelazione termografica di difetti nei dipinti," *La Termotecnica* 33, no. 12: 643-50), that these conditions represent no damage to the "delicati rivetimenti portanti dal muro." The heat reemitted under low-heat flow conditions is very different according to the nature of the plaster-wall masonry interface. In detached areas the heat remains longer and a white zone is observed in a picture of the image taken during the reemission stage.

Although no data about the nature, composition, and thickness of the plaster are reported in the paper, it can be assumed that in contrast with the tomb of Nefertari the plaster was more or less uniform in thickness. In addition, the plaster-masonry wall interface was flat and parallel to the outer wall surface. All these considerations imply that the church of Sant'Angelo is significantly different from the tomb of Nefertari where the rough plaster-rock interface makes echo monitoring difficult. Therefore, the positive results obtained with this procedure in the church of Sant'Angelo may not be expected in the study of the tomb of Nefertari.

Condition Survey

Paolo and Laura Mora
Lorenza D'Alessandro
Giorgio Capriotti

The discovery of the tomb of Nefertari posed an extremely complex conservation problem. Schiaparelli described the precarious conditions in which the wall paintings appeared from the moment of their discovery, and provided information of the initial indispensable restoration interventions made by Prof. Lucarini. Around 1930 the Metropolitan Museum of Art sponsored a complete photographic documentation of all the painted surfaces, excluding the ceiling. Just before World War II the Egyptian authorities, in order to prevent any further decay to the tomb, closed it to the public. Since that time, the tomb has been the subject of studies by numerous experts. The conservation of the tomb of Nefertari has therefore always been, for the Egyptian authorities, a prevailing problem that, with well justified caution, they have postponed solving until today.

Aware of the fragility of the tomb and complex nature of the setting, the Egyptian authorities did not wish to approach any conservation attempt without having previously obtained data through a systematic and thorough study absolutely guaranteeing a positive result.

At the end of 1986, the Egyptian Antiquities Organization in collaboration with the Getty Conservation Institute decided with great courage to face up to the problem in a resolute and systematic manner and to establish a multidisciplinary program using the most precise study methodologies and research technology to determine the basic framework of the intervention for the tomb of Nefertari, consisting of: (1) archaeological analysis, technological analysis, analysis of the alterations and their etiology, and other forms of analysis; (2) graphic documentation, photographic documentation, and other forms of documentation; (3) processing of the information and diagnosis of the first phase; (4) project design of the final total conservation.

Parallel to the studies in point 1, it was necessary to activate the gathering of documentation to obtain a complete view of the parameters. These would be used to determine the present condition and would also guide further studies.

The state of conservation of a work is the result of a synthesis of the collected data plus a critical reading of the surface. To compile this synthesis it is necessary to have direct knowledge of the constituent materials and execution techniques and an analytical verification of their reactions to the different decay phenomena. In this way it is possible to describe the state of conservation as it relates specifically to the nature, history, and condition of the work.

In the tomb of Nefertari the particularly complex phenomenology of the decay required readings at four different levels: (1) the condition of the support; (2) alterations of the painted layer; (3) typology and location of foreign substances; and (4) previous interventions.

For the survey of the state of conservation of the support, six different types of decays were individually identified: (1) cracks (fissures or fractures in the rock structure or in the stratifications of the plaster); (2) extrusion of rock chips (geological dislocations of the rock); (3) separation of the plaster (reduction of the adhesion of the plaster, of various types at different levels); (4) lack of cohesion of the plaster (tendency to the disaggregation of the preparatory strata); (5)lacunae of depth (loss of the entire stratification); and (6) lacunae of surface (loss of the surface plaster).

The alterations of the painted surfaces identified were: (1) lack of cohesion of the painted layer (trend to pigment pulverization); (2) detachment of the pictorial layer (flaking of the color); (3) loss of the pictorial layer; (4) abrasion (direct mechanical damage, wear); (5) macular chromatic alterations (evident smear of the color tone of the painted surface); and (6) natural deposits (earth sediment and dust, insect nests).

The salts appeared under two forms: (1) macroscopic subflorescence (salt crystallization of special eruptive and damaging capacity); and (2) efflorescence (specific salt crystallization on the painted surface).

To determine the previous interventions a visual survey was conducted of the following categories: (1) fillings of lacunae (fillings of lacunae at surface and subsurface levels); (2) splashings of filling mortars (residues of interventions of fillings of lacunae); (3) overpaintings (pictorial restoration done on the fillings); (4) retouches (pictorial restoration done on the original); (5) surface treatments (residuals of conservation fixers); (6) shifted colors; (7) facings (gauze and scotch tape applied to block endangered areas); and (8) detached fragments replaced in situ.

To compile the survey schemes it was necessary to photograph the entire tomb in black and white at 1:10 scale to allow sufficiently accurate analytical reading of the decay. In the survey phase to permit faster consultation of the data tables themselves, the photographic reproductions were reduced to scale 1:20. The identification of the various surroundings and individual walls were processed from the surveys and maps already published at 1:50 scale.

On every photograph four transparent acetate sheets were superimposed for the four levels of readings already indicated, relative to the state of conservation of the paintings. For every item of the schemes graphic symbols were added with color markers, showing the localization of the phenomena of degradation. The punctual and analytical survey of these phenomena was done manually with the aid of cold lights in direct and raking light and with stereoscopic enlargement lenses in the entire surface of the tomb (about 520m²). The survey operations were conducted in situ in this manner, and the graphic work was continued in Rome. From the photos the wall painting designs were replicated in scale on the transparent sheets that had supplied the graphic base for the succeeding surveys. The linear synthesis adopted in the designs responds to the precise demands of visual reference and does not represent iconographical accuracy.

From transparent sheet bases four copies on nonmodifiable photographic paper in a 50 x 70 cm format were obtained. On the copies of every base the relevant data was reported with specific symbols. The choice of colors, referring to the single phenomenon of degradation, responds to a precise perceptual code; for example, the color red always indicates an emergency situation (detachment of the plaster or flaking of pictorial layer).

About two hundred tables were composed, complete with titles, topographic references, and scale, to supply a complete picture of the present condition of the paintings in the tomb of Nefertari. In a separate photographic album the captions of the four levels of conservation surveys were reported, accompanied by explanatory photographic references, which are indispensable for an immediate visualization of the various types of alteration.

Figure 1. A systematic and detailed visual inspection of the tomb was done in preparation of the condition survey work.

From the resulting data following the first cross-referenced survey the emergency situations were identified. The interdisciplinary nature of the group made possible the definition of an emergency consolidation. A characteristic of this emergency condition is the possibility of an immediate reversible treatment, not only technological but also conceptual. The reversibility of this emergency consolidation has a thermodynamic dimension that is done gradually in such a way that it is possible to either stop or invert the alteration actions of the conservation.

Of primary importance are the processing and cross referencing of the data produced by hand, to ensure that they do not remain as elaborate monographs without any practical application.

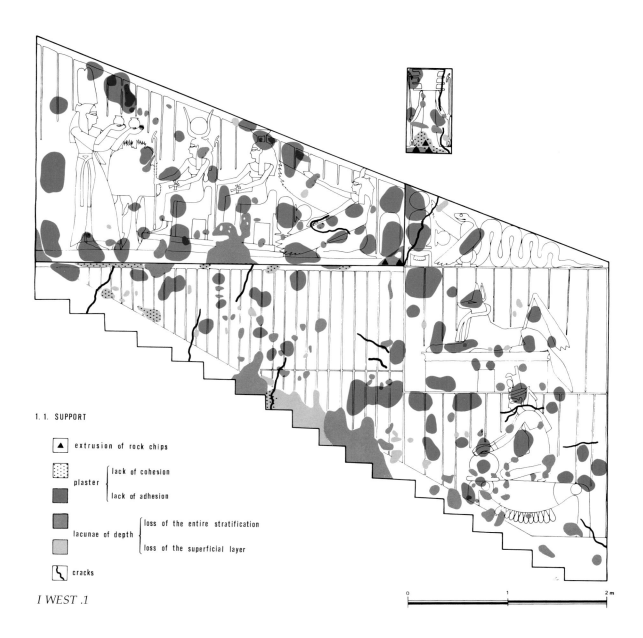

1. 1. SUPPORT

▲ extrusion of rock chips

plaster ⎰ lack of cohesion
        ⎱ lack of adhesion

lacunae of depth ⎰ loss of the entire stratification
                 ⎱ loss of the superficial layer

cracks

I WEST .1

Figure 2-13. This sequence of photographs shows the four levels of reading and their related problems done for each wall in the tomb as well as the identification of those areas in urgent need of conservation.

1.2. PAINT LAYER

⬚ lack of cohesion

■ flaking

⬚ abrasions

⩒ loss of paint layer

▦ natural deposits { earth sediments and dust
△   { insect broods

▨ macular chromatic alterations

I WEST .2

0   1   2 m

1.3. CRYSTALLIZATION SALTS

☐ macroscopic sub-florescences

■ efflorescences

I WEST .3

0   1   2 m

1. 4. PREVIOUS INTERVENTIONS

fillings of lacunae

retouches

over-paintings

shifted colors

surface treatments

facings (gauze – scotch)

spreading of filling mortars

I WEST .4

0   1   2 m

G EAST .1

G EAST .2

G EAST .3

0   1   2 m.

G EAST .4

0   1   2 m.

C WEST .1

0   1   2m

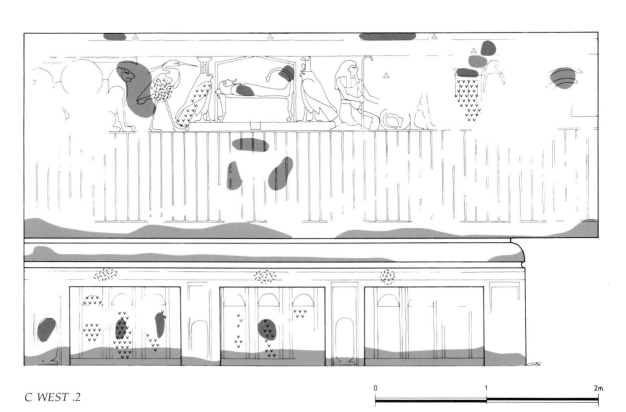

C WEST .2

0   1   2m

C WEST .3

0   1   2m.

C WEST .4

0   1   2m.

الاختبار الغير متلف

دكتور مودستو مونتوتو
رئيس قسم البترولوجيا
جامعة أفييدو ـ أسبانيا

تركز هذه الدراسة على إيجاد طريقة لرصد أماكن الفراغات خلف الطبقة الحاملة للون التي تبدو سليمة وذلك لتشخيص حالة التحامها أو عدمه مع الصخر .

يعزى الانفصال بين طبقة الملاط والصخر داخل مقبرة نفرتاري إلى تبلور الملح بينهما مما سبب ضغوطاً ميكانيكية أدت الى تكوين فراغات بين الملاط والصخر .

لم نجد طريقة ـ غير متلفة ـ مثلى استخدمت من قبل لتطبيقها في مقبرة نفرتاري ، ومع ذلك فقد قدمنا وصفاً لمتطلبات إجراء اختبار غير متلف والتي تنحصر في العديد من الاحداثيات مثل رجع الصدى ، الذبذبات ... الخ . ملحق بهذا البحث ثبت مراجع .

مسح حالة المقبرة

باولـــو مـــورا
مرمم خاص
روما ـ إيطاليا

تمت عملية المسح الشامل لحالة النقوش الجدارية لمقبرة نفرتاري في شهري أكتوبر ونوفمبر ١٩٨٦ بالاشتراك مع هيئة الآثار المصرية وفريق من المرممين . لقد ركز المسح على الفحص المتأني للطبقة الحاملة للألوان ولطبقة الألوان نفسها ولتبلور الملح وكذلك للمحاولات السابقة للترميم .

لقد استخدمت الصور التي قدمها مركز تسجيل الآثار ـ هيئة الآثار المصرية ـ وكذلك بعض الصور التي تطلبتها عملية المسح كخلفية وقع عليها الظروف المختلفة لاحداثيات النقوش الجدارية . بعد إتمام هذه العملية ترجمت هذه المعلومات رسومات مبسطة للنقوش الجدارية استخدم فيها الأكواد اللونية والرمزية .

تمثل هذه الدراسة تسجيلا منظماً ومنسقاً ولقد ساعد هذا كثيرا في فهم مشاكل النقوش الجدارية وفي التوصل الى قرار بخصوص إنتخاب بعضها للترميم العاجل .

التقرير الأول عن تحاليل العينات

دكتور فرانك برويسر

مدير البرنامج العلمي

معهد جيتى للصيانة

ملخــص

أجريت تحاليل مختلفة ـ استخدم فيها ، الفحص المجهري ، حيود الاشعة السينية ، والحزمة الالكترونية ـ على عينات من الملح ، الملاط ، الألوان ، و « الجبس » أستجلبت من مقبرة ملاصقة لمقبرة نفرتاري . وقد أكدت نتائج هذه التحاليل ما توصل اليه بحاث سابقون بالنسبة للملح (كلوريد الصوديوم) ، والملاط (جير مطفي ، و « جبس » ، وطفلة) والألوان . ولقد جمعت نتائج إضافية وصممت خطة عمل سيجرى تنفيذها مستقبلا .

الألوان ، الملاط ، وتحاليل الملح

صالح أحمد صالح

رئيس قسم الصيانة

كلية علم الآثار

جامعة القاهرة

لقد استخدمت عدة طرق (الأشعة السينية ، والأشعة التنويرية ، وتحاليل كيميائية رطبة والفحص المجهري) لتحليل المواد المستعملة في النقوش الجدارية لمقبرة نفرتاري .

لقد ظهرت نتائج تحاليل الألوان والملاط و بلورات الملح .

المسح الميكرومناخي داخل مقبرة نفرتاري

د / فيصل عبدالحليم اسماعيل

كانت الظروف البيئية الداخلية أول عناصر البحث التي اتجهت اليها أنظار الدارسين لحالة مقبرة نفرتاري من الحفظ ، وتقييم امكانيات العلاج . و يأتي هذا نتيجة الجفاف الملحوظ بها ، والذي يعتبر عاملا أساسياً في نمو البللورات الملحية من المحاليل المشبعة التي نفذت في القديم خلال نسيج الصخر .. إلى السطح الداخلي للمقبرة ، فأحدثت ذلك التلف الواقع في نسبة كبيرة من النقوش الجدارية . ومن أجل هذا جرى قياس أو تسجيل ، عاملين مناخيين مترابطين ورئيسيين ... هما درجة الحرارة والرطوبة النسبية لجو المقبرة وان يكون على درجات متباعدة .

منذ بداية الدراسات العلمية بالمقبرة عام ١٩٥٨ وحتى عام ١٩٧٦ ولكننا نجد على كل حال أنه منذ نهاية ١٩٧٧ زاد عدد مرات القياس للعام مثلما ان التسجيل قد امتد لفترات طويلة حيث بلغت نحو ستة اشهر عام ١٩٨١ ثم من سبتمبر ١٩٨٦ حتى مارس ١٩٨٧ في نطاق الدراسات الحاضرة .

ولعل من أهم ما خرج به المسح الميكرومناخي الجاري ما يلي :

١ – تتراوح درجات الحرارة داخل المقبرة بين ٢٦م ، ٣٠م وتتراوح الرطوبة النسبية بين ٢٠٪ ، ٤٥٪ .

٢ – تتغير العوامل الميكرومناخية المقاسة بدرجة منظورة موسميا .

٣ – تبقى درجة الحرارة ثابتة (تقريبا) خلال الموسم المعين ، بينما تتغير الرطوبة النسبية فتصبح بهذا العامل المناخي الحرج والمؤثر في حالة الحفظ للمقبرة .

قياسات الألوان

لفرانك برو يسر ومايكل شيلنج
معهد جيتى للصيانة

كان الغرض من إجراء قياسات الألوان في مقبرة نفرتاري هو الحصول على سجل دقيق لألوان النقوش الجدارية المختلفة قبيل صيانتها ، وقد أختيرت أماكن القياسات داخل المقبرة بحيث تمثل درجات الحفظ المختلفة لهذه النقوش والتي تتدرج بين الجيد والمتدهور الذي يتكون من بقايا ملاط ملون ردىء الحفظ . أجريت هذه القياسات باستخدام كروما متر معدل (مينولتا سي . آر– ١٢١) مع داتا بروسسر (دي . بي – ١٠٠) على سبع لوحات جدارية داخل المقبرة حيث قيست جميع الألوان الموجودة في كل لوحة . سجلت أماكن القياسات بواسطة التصوير الفوتوغرافي منسوباً الى منظور المقبرة .

أجريت التحاليل الكيميائية والفيزيائية على عينات من الملاط الملون وغير الملون والملح والتي كانت موجودة في صناديق تخزين داخل المقبرة . وزودت المقبرة بأجهزة لقياس الرطوبة والحرارة في ثلاثة أماكن داخل المقبرة ، ونتائج هذه الدراسات يتضمنها هذا الكتاب .

المحتوى الجغرافي والجيولوجي لمقبرة نفرتاري

للدكتور فاروق الباز
مدير مركز الاستشعار من بعد
جامعة بوسطن

يصف هذا المقال نتائج المسح الأولى لمنطقة المقبرة والذي ينحصر في إستخدام الصور الفضائية المعالجة بواسطة الحساب الآلي والتحليل الضوئي للحصول على خرائط دقيقة لأنماط التراكيب الجيولوجية وللمجاري الطبيعية للصرف ، والتي وجد انها تتبع ثلاثة اتجاهات رئيسية : شمال شرق ــ جنوب غرب ، شمال غرب ــ جنوب شرق و شرق ــ غرب و ينبغي التنوية هنا أن في عملية تصريف المياه التي تسقط أحيانا في منطقة المقبرة تتبع مجاري دقيقة تحددها طوبوغرافية موقع المقبرة . وقد لوحظ ان الحجر الجيري المنحوت فيه مقبرة نفرتاري والمقبرتين الملاصقتين لها قد تعرض لعملية تفلق أدت الى وجد الكثير من الفوالق المتصلة والمملوءة ببلورات الجبس الليفية والمتعامدة على مستوى هذه الفوالق وكذلك ببلورات الملح الصخري . ولقد سببت الأخيرة انفصال طبقة الملاط عن سطح صخر المقبرة في النهاية .

ومن أجل التوصل الى تفهم أعمق لظروف المقبرة فانه رؤي عمل خرائط طبوغرافية وتركيبية للموقع وتحديد مجاري الصرف وكذلك تعيين العامود الاستراتيجرافي لصخور المقبرة وعمل نماذج إمتثال هيدرولوجية المنطقة وكذلك لتبلور الملح .

الفحوص البيولوجية

هيديو أرائي
رئيس وحدة الأبحاث البيولوجية
قسم علم المحافظة على الآثار
معهد طوكيو القومي لبحوث المقتنيات الثقافية

لاحظ المؤلف وجود بعض الحشرات النشطة وكذلك بقايا بعض القوارض كما أن جفاف المقبرة (٣٠ ــ ٤٠٪ نسبة الرطوبة) قد أثار إنتباهه . إن تحول لون سقف الغرفتين الجانبيتين (الغربية M ، والشرقية O) من اللون الأزرق الى اللون الأسود قد يكون سببه كائنات حية دقيقة .

لقد مسحت المقبرة ــ ميكرو بيولوجياً ــ مرتين ، الأولى قبل أن يطأها فريق الاخصائيين والأخرى بعد ذلك ، وقد تمت عملية المسح بأخذ مسحات من هواء المقبرة .

لقد أظهر العد الفطري والبكتيري أن هنالك مساواة في توزيع هذه الأعداد قبل دخول فريق الخبراء المقبرة ، ولكن هذا العد تضاعف بعد دخول فريق الخبراء .

وأكثر نتيجة ملفتة للنظر وجود (كلادوسبوريوم) في المسحات الهوائية التي أخذت بعد دخول فريق الخبراء المقبرة والتي كانت منعدمة قبل ذلك .

الجهود السابقة في محاولة علاج مقبرة نفرتاري

د / أحـمـد قـدري

د / فيصل عبدالحليم اسماعيل

أكتشفت المقبرة خلال أعمال حفائر المجموعة الايطالية بقيادة «اسكياباريللي» بين عامي ١٩٠٣، ١٩٢٠ و يشير التقرير الأول للحملة الى فداحة التلف الذي قد أصاب قدرا من النقوش الجدارية بها . ولزم القيام بأعمال ترميم عاجلة في حينه ، لم يوضح التقرير طبيعتها أو درجتها . و يرجع هذا في الغالب إلى حقيقة أن تلك المرحلة المبكرة من الاستكشافات الأثرية لـم تكـن تعني بالتوثيق الكامل الذي نشترطه اليوم في النشاطات الحفرية . ولهذا السبب ذاته فاننا نفتقد البيان المسجل بأعمال ترميم تبعت ، قامت بها مصلحة الآثار المصرية قبل و بعد الحرب العالمية الثانية .

وهكذا اعتمـد منهـاج العمل في البداية على التدخل المباشر والتجربة والخطأ ثم تطور أسلوب التناول إلى إجراء تجارب عملية أولية محدودة بالمقبرة .

ومع تحول الفن الفطري والتقليدي للترميم إلى علم صيانة جامع ، أصبح لزاما أن يسبق التدخل العلاجي فحوصات عـمـليـة حقلية ومعملية ينبني على أساس من نتائجها أي علاج يتقرر للأثر . وأعتمد الأسلوب العلمي منهاجا للتعامل مع مشاكل إدارة وصيانة الكيان الأثري لا يمكن ولا يصح ، الحيود عنه .

وحظيت مقبرة نفرتاري بأكبر الاهتمام من المنظمات والمؤسسات العلمية المحلية والعالمية . وكانت منظمة «اليونسكو» سباقة في إرسال بعثاتها العلمية والفنية لدراسة حالة مقبرة نفرتاري أعوام ١٩٥٨، ١٩٦٩، ١٩٧٠ . وأصبح تقرير البعثة الأخيرة مرجعاً أساسياً لما قد تبعه من دراسات بالمقبرة ، والتي اجرتها مجموعات بحثية وفنية متخصصة من بولندا (١٩٧٣) ، الايكروم (١٩٧٨) ، جامعة القاهرة (١٩٨٠) ، كندا (١٩٧٧ – ١٩٨١) ، وإيطاليا (١٩٨٣) ... إلى أن بلغ الجهد الدولي المباشر مبتغاه مع بداية العمل المتكامل الحاضر، في نطاق التعاون المشترك بين هيئة الآثار المصرية ومعهد جيتى الأمريكي للصيانة .

النقوش الجدارية لمقبرة نفرتاري

تقـــديم

أثارت النقوش الجدارية لمقبرة نفرتاري منذ اكتشفها إسكيا باريللي عام ١٩٠٤ إنتباه العلماء والمتخصصين وعامة الناس وذلك نظراً لأهميتها التاريخية وقيمتها الجمالية النادرة . ولكنها أصبحت محور قلق أخصائي الصيانة نظراً لحالتها الحرجة والخطر الوشيك الذي يتمثل في تدهورها وفقدانها .

يعرض هذا الكتاب المجهودات التي بذلت منذ شهر سبتمبر ١٩٨٦ في الدراسة والبحث وإجراء التحاليل وذلك لتحديد مسار العمل بالنسبة لتقوية وتثبيت النقوش الجدارية بصفة عاجلة ، ولاختيار أنسب الطرق لترميمها ومعالجتها .

إنطلاقا من حرص كل من هيئة الآثار المصرية ومعهد جيتي للصيانة على المحافظة على التراث الثقافي ، قررا المبادرة ببدء مشروع مشترك لايجاد أفضل الطرق لانقاذ النقوش الجدارية لمقبرة نفرتاري من استمرار تدهورها . ومن أجل ذلك قامت الهيئتان بدعوة فريق عمل من الأخصائيين المصريين والأجانب من مختلف التخصصات للمشاركة في هذا العمل الهام . ولقد ابتدأ المشروع بدراسة صور معززة أخذت من مركبة فضاء وذلك لفهم جيولوجية منطقة الأقصر و بالتحديد وادي الملكات في البر الغربي لنهر النيل . ولقد شكلت الدراسات البيولوجية والكيميائية والفيزيائية والترميمية جزءاً متكاملا من البرنامج العام للدراسة الشاملة لمشاكل المقبرة وذلك لضمان نجاح المشروع .

وتمثل الأبحاث التي يتضمنها هذا الكتاب ما تم تنفيذه في هذا الصدد حتى الآن . يدرك كل من هيئة الآثار المصرية ومعهد جيتي للصيانة ان هذه الدراسات تمثل مرحلة أولى سيتبعها بالضرورة أعمال مكثفة .

ويحدونا الأمل في أن هذا التقرير المرحلي الأول سوف يستحوذ على إنتباه كل المهتمين بصيانة التراث الثقافي على وجه العموم والنقوش الجدارية لمقبرة نفرتاري على وجه الخصوص .

دكتور أحمد قدري	السيد / لويس مونريال
رئيس هيئة الآثار المصرية	مدير معهد جيتى للصيانة

دكتور / فاروق الباز

مدير مركز الأستشعار من بعد

جامعة بوسطون

بوسطون ، مساتشوستس ، أميركا

دكتور / محمد الصغير

مدير عام آثار الأقصر

هيئة الآثار المصرية

الأقصر ، مصر

دكتور / جاب الله علي جاب الله

وكيل كلية الآثار

جامعة القاهرة

الجيزة ، مصر

دكتور / هاني حمروش

قسم الجيولوجيا

كلية العلوم ـ جامعة القاهرة

الجيزة ، مصر

دكتور / مدستو منتوتو

رئيس قسم البترولوجي

جامعة أفييدو، أسبانيا

الاستاذ / باولو مورا

رئيس المرممين «سابقا»

المعهد المركزي للترميم

روما ، إيطاليا

دكتور / شوقي نخله

مدير عام قسم ترميم الآثار المصرية

هيئة الآثار المصرية

القاهرة ، مصر

السيد / محمد نصر

رئيس مفتشي القرنة

الأقصر ، مصر

دكتور / فرانك برو يسر

مدير البرنامج العلمي

معهد جيتى للصيانة

مرينا دل راي ، كاليفورنيا ، أميركا

دكتورة / وفاء الصديق

مديرة الأمانة العلمية للآثار المصرية

هيئة الآثار المصرية

القاهرة ، مصر

دكتور / صالح أحمد صالح

رئيس قسم الترميم

كلية الآثار، جامعة القاهرة

القاهرة ، مصر

السيد / مايكل شيلنج

باحث مساعد

معهد جيتى للصيانة

مرينا دل راي ، كاليفورنيا ، أميركا

أفراد المشروع

دكتور / أحمد قدري
رئيس هيئة الآثار المصرية
القاهرة ، مصر

دكتور / جمال مختار
الرئيس الأسبق لهيئة الآثار المصرية
القاهرة ، مصر

السيد / لويس مونريال
مدير معهد جيتى للصيانة
مرينا دل راي ، كاليفورنيا ، أميركا

دكتور / فيصل عبدالحليم اسماعيل
مستشار في صيانة وحفظ الآثار
هيئة الآثار المصرية
القاهرة ، مصر

مهندس / فرج عبدالمطلب
مدير الشئون الهندسية
الأقصر ، مصر

مهندس / نبيل عبدالسميع
مدير عام الشئون الهندسية
هيئة الآثار المصرية
القاهرة ، مصر

الأستاذ / هيديو أرائي
رئيس ، وحدة بحوث البيولوجيا
قسم علم المحافظة على الآثار
معهد طوكيو القومي لبحوث المقتنيات الثقافية
طوكيو ، اليابان

السيد / جييرمو ألدانا
خبير تصوير فوتوجرافي
ميكسيكو سيتي ، المكسيك

السيد / مطاوع بلبوش
مدير عام المناطق الأثرية لمصر العليا
هيئة الآثار المصرية
القاهرة ، مصر

دكتور / كمال بركات
مدير عام مركز البحوث والصيانة
هيئة الآثار المصرية
القاهرة ، مصر

دكتور / مجل أنجل كورسو
مكتب المدير لتنمية المشروعات
معهد جيتى للصيانة
مرينا دل راي ، كاليفورنيا ، أميركا

دكتور / عمر العريني
مستشار الشئون العلمية
الهيئة القومية للعلوم ومدير المشروع
القاهرة ، مصر

النقوش الجدارية لمقبرة نفرتاري

المحتويات

أفراد المشروع

النقوش الجدارية لمقبرة نفرتاري
تقـــديم

دكتور أحمد قدري
رئيس هيئة الآثار المصرية

السيد / لويس مونريال
مدير معهد جيتى للصيانة

الجهود السابقة في محاولة علاج مقبرة نفرتاري

د / أحـــمـــد قـــدري
د / فيصل عبدالحليم اسماعيل

المحتوى الجغرافي والجيولوجي لمقبرة نفرتاري

للدكتور فاروق الباز
مدير مركز الاستشعار من بعد
جامعة بوسطن

الفحوص البيولوجية

هيديو أرائي
رئيس وحدة الأبحاث البيولوجية
قسم علم المحافظة على الآثار
معهد طوكيو القومي لبحوث المقتنيات الثقافية

المسح الميكرومناخي داخل مقبرة نفرتاري

د / فيصل عبدالحليم اسماعيل

قياسات الألـــوان

لفرانك برويسر ومايكل شيلنج
معهد جيتى للصيانة

التقرير الأول عن تحاليل العينات

دكتور فرانك برويسر
مدير البرنامج العلمي
معهد جيتى للصيانة

الألوان ، الملاط ، وتحاليل الملح

صالح أحمد صالح
رئيس قسم الصيانة
كلية علم الآثار
جامعة القاهرة

الاختبار الغير متلف

دكتور مودستو مونتوتو
رئيس قسم البترولوجيا
جامعة أفييدو ـ أسبانيا

مسح حالة المقبرة

باولـــو مـــورا
مرمم خاص
روما ـ إيطاليا

النقوش الجدارية لمقبرة نفرتاري

الدراسات العلمية لصيانتها

التقرير المرحلي الأول

يولية ١٩٨٧

مشروع مشترك

بين

هيئة الآثار المصرية

و

معهد جيتى للصيانة

مطبوعات هيئة الآثار المصرية

حَوليّاتَ هيئة الآثار المصرية

النقوش الجدارية لمقبرة نفرتاري